Stand Up For Yourself, Set Boundaries, & Stop Pleasing Others
(if that's okay with you...)

By Patrick King
Social Interaction and Conversation Coach at
www.PatrickKingConsulting.com

Table of Contents

PART 1: WHY ARE SOME PEOPLE PEOPLE-PLEASERS? 9

CHAPTER 1: THE NEED TO BE LIKED 11

- YOU'RE AN INK BLOT — 17
- YOUR WORTH DOES NOT COME FROM OTHERS' APPROVAL — 18
- THERE'S NOTHING WRONG WITH HAVING NEEDS—AND MEETING THEM — 19
- YOU ARE NOT OMNIPOTENT — 21
- THE "SEPARATION OF TASKS" EXERCISE — 22

CHAPTER 2: ARE YOU GENEROUS? OR JUST AFRAID OF REJECTION? 27

- HOW TO BREAK THE FEAR OF REJECTION CYCLE — 31
- HAVE SELF-COMPASSION — 37
- CHALLENGE YOUR NARRATIVES — 38
- FOCUS ON PROCESS AND NOT OUTCOME — 39

CHAPTER 3: "FAWNING"—A RESPONSE TO TRAUMA 41

- GET PROFESSIONAL HELP — 45
- REPARENT YOURSELF — 45
- RECONNECT WITH YOUR PRINCIPLES AND VALUES — 47
- BECOME AN EXPERT ON YOUR OWN FEELINGS — 48
- HAVE FUN! — 50

CHAPTER 4: WHY CONFLICT AVOIDANCE IS ACTUALLY A HIGH-RISK STRATEGY   53

THE TERRIBLE TALE OF THE "GUNNYSACK"	56
BUT... WHAT'S THE ALTERNATIVE?	57

PART 2: THE PEOPLE-PLEASER'S SURVIVAL KIT   67

CHAPTER 5: SIX DIFFERENT WAYS TO SAY NO   69

DIRECT NO	70
REASONED NO	70
REFLECTING NO	71
RAINCHECK NO	72
ENQUIRING NO	73
BROKEN RECORD NO	74
CHALLENGING THE BELIEFS THAT STOP YOU FROM SAYING NO	77

CHAPTER 6: EVERYONE NEEDS BOUNDARIES... INCLUDING YOU!   81

REFRAME WHAT YOU ARE KEEPING OUT WITH YOUR BOUNDARY	84
TRUST YOUR FEELINGS	86
RESPECT OTHER PEOPLE'S BOUNDARIES	87
GIVE UP EXPLAINING	89
FOLLOW UP WITH ACTION	90

CHAPTER 7: BEING ASSERTIVE—OR AT LEAST HOW TO FAKE IT TILL YOU MAKE IT   95

WATCH YOUR BODY LANGUAGE	100

MAINTAIN COMFORTABLE EYE CONTACT ... 101
DRESS THE PART ... 102
DEVELOP YOUR PERSONAL SENSE OF POISE ... 103

CHAPTER 8: ASSERTIVE COMMUNICATION—SPEAK LOUD, SPEAK CLEAR, AND SPEAK FROM THE HEART ... 105

FEELINGS ARE NEVER RIGHT OR WRONG ... 107
PEOPLE ARE RESPONSIBLE FOR THEIR OWN FEELINGS ... 109
UNDERSTAND WHAT THE GOAL OF COMMUNICATION IS ... 111
APPLYING SELF-KNOWLEDGE AND ASKING FOR WHAT YOU WANT ... 112

PART 3: CHANGING YOUR MINDSET FOR GOOD ... 119

CHAPTER 10: DON'T TAKE YOUR INNER CRITIC'S WORD FOR IT ... 121

"IS THE CHOICE I'M MAKING FOR ME OR FOR SOMEONE ELSE?" ... 124
"IS MY INNER CRITIC WORKING FOR ME OR AGAINST ME?" ... 125
"WHAT IS MY INNER CRITIC TRYING TO ACHIEVE?" ... 127

CHAPTER 11: HOW TO DROP THE PEOPLE-PLEASER'S WORST HABIT—OVER-APOLOGIZING ... 131

CHAPTER 12: PLUGGING INTO THE ENERGY SOURCE OF SELF-VALIDATION ... 143

STEP 1: BE AWARE OF WHAT YOU FEEL ... 146
STEP 2: NORMALIZE ... 149
STEP 3: TELL THE TRUTH ... 151

PART 4: KIND AND COMPASSIONATE... BUT NOT A DOORMAT! — 157

CHAPTER 13: THE ART OF COMPASSION... REAL COMPASSION — 159

Mindfulness Meditation for People-Pleasers — 160
Loving-Kindness Meditation for People-Pleasers — 165

CHAPTER 14: BREAKING THE ILLUSORY BONDS OF CODEPENDENCY — 171

Make Yourself Your New Rescue Project — 175

CHAPTER 15: CHARTING YOUR PROGRESS IN BLACK AND WHITE — 183

Use a Journal and Be Your Own Therapist — 185
How to Use Affirmations — 188

SUMMARY GUIDE — 199

Part 1: Why are Some People People-Pleasers?

Chapter 1: The Need to be Liked

"Hey, could you stay late this evening and finish up all my work for me? There's a party tonight and I'll miss it if I don't leave now."

"Oh sure! Of course! Uh . . . do you need me to give you a lift there?"

People call them doormats, pushovers, or people-pleasers, but whatever they're called, they all seem to have the same playbook: be nice, be helpful, be kind, and no matter what you do, never *ever* say no.

In this book, we'll be looking closely at the seemingly irresistible need to please others at all costs and how to tackle the sometimes devastating effects of putting yourself last. We'll look at *why* you might be a people-pleaser and what lies at the root of your mindset. This way, you can begin unpicking certain core beliefs so that you're empowered to set healthier boundaries and start to take charge of your life.

People may tell you, "Just say no! Just be firm!" but the truth is, if you're a chronic people-pleaser, it goes a lot deeper than this. We'll explore some easy tips and tricks to "fake it 'til you make it," but we'll also take a closer look at how to make more lasting and fundamental changes. These changes will help you genuinely feel more content, composed, and confident in yourself so that you truly don't *need* to people-please anymore.

A wonderful thing happens when people give up people-pleasing: they realize that when they're happy, balanced, and assertive, their relationships are actually more respectful, more intimate, and more real—not less!

People-pleasing is a complex learned behavior, but the good news is that with a little effort, you can shift your mindset and start to engage with others on more genuine, mature, and equal footing. No matter where you are right now, this book will show you how.

One major cause of people-pleasing is the need to be liked.

Are you a people-pleaser? Chances are you already know the answer to this question, but there is one tell-tale sign that may reveal a deeper problem: you constantly think, "I wonder if they like me?"

Do they like how I look?

Do they like my work?

Do they think I'm interesting or intelligent or valuable?

Am I needed?

Do they like what I say or what I do?

*Do they like **me**?*

First things first: wanting to be liked is not a problem. It's human. We all seek out acceptance into a group and try hard to avoid being rejected. Humans evolved in small tribes in which being a part of the bigger whole was necessary for survival.

Therefore, there's nothing intrinsically wrong with caring about the opinions of others, wanting their validation, or feeling good about yourself because they feel good about you.

The trouble is, a people-pleaser can have difficulty finding where to draw the line between this need to please and their own need for authenticity, dignity, and self-worth. In other words, it's a problem of balance.

There are people out there who don't consider the opinions of others *enough*—they may be callous, inconsiderate, uncaring, or outright hostile to the idea of pleasing other people. But if you're reading this book, chances are that you fall on the other end of the spectrum. When it comes to your own self-concept and worth as a human being, you give the opinions and actions of others too much weight.

Here are a few examples in which the need to people-please has tipped over from a normal human desire into a set of behaviors that actively limits life's potential:

- You submit a project to a client who usually gives you effusive praise, only to have them say, "Thanks!" and move on without a second thought. You spend all evening wondering what they really think and whether they actually hated the project or worse, whether it's *you* they hate.
- You accidentally said something offensive and immediately apologized. The other person is a bit hurt but has forgiven you and appears to have moved on. However, you find yourself wracked with guilt and can't stop thinking of things you should be doing to make it up to them. You keep apologizing until the whole situation is awkward.
- You're dating someone new, and all your focus immediately goes to finding out what they like so you can be that. You subtly alter how you speak, dress, or behave in an unconscious bid to be the kind of person you hope they'll be attracted to.

Dr. Roger Covin is a clinical psychologist and author of the book *The Need to be Liked*. His research has shown him that although people-pleasing has roots in natural human social behavior, it can cause a few problems:

It can stop you from doing what you want (because what will they think?).

It can stop you from exploring, creating, or trying something new (too risky).

It can cause anxiety and unhappiness.

Basically, if your life's purpose is meeting the needs of other people, then what happens to *your* needs? A people-pleasing life is often inauthentic, stressful, and unhappy. At the core of this life are two lies: the first is that it is one hundred percent totally and absolutely unacceptable for us to be disliked. The second is that it is our job to make other people happy, and that we are responsible for how they feel.

How do we let go of these lies? Here are the insights and attitudes associated with a healthier sense of self.

You're an Ink Blot

Think of a Rorschach ink blot test. Everyone sees in those ambiguous blobs whatever they want to see. And what they see has nothing to do with the blob itself. Think of yourself the same way!

Some people will like you, and some won't. Some people will love certain characteristics in you, while others hate those same traits. And it doesn't mean a thing. If someone says, "I like you," it's not all that different from them saying "I prefer strawberry ice cream to chocolate." There's no judgment, and nothing is wrong. The person is simply telling you their opinion, which is their business. In other words, a person saying "I don't like you" is not a problem to solve, a mistake, a crisis, or an insult.

You might go on a date with a woman who announces that she doesn't like skinny men. You, being a skinny man, could think either 1) "I should bulk up at the gym or women won't like me," or 2) "Oh well, I guess we're not compatible!"

There are seven billion people on this earth. Can you even imagine the type of person you'd need to be to win *everyone's* approval? It's impossible.

Your Worth Does Not Come from Others' Approval

For our ancient ancestors, being expelled from the group may literally have meant death. For modern, evolved humankind—not so much.

It's normal to occasionally meet disapproval. Really! If you think about it, you probably cannot think of a single person out there who hasn't been disapproved of by someone else at some point. And you probably disapprove of many others! People-pleasers may dwell on the agonizing question, "Why don't they like me?!" but really, does the answer matter? Can we have the courage to recognize that even if someone doesn't like us, we don't vanish in a puff of smoke? We are still who we are, and our happiness is still what we make of it.

A healthy mindset assures us that our self-worth does not come from the (fleeting, potentially flawed) opinions and tastes of others. You may choose a career path that your family despises, for example, but makes you happy. With a healthy mindset, though, you can tell yourself, "I have worth whether or not they approve."

Who says you can't live a happy, healthy, meaningful, and awesome life while at the same time, some people dislike you?

There's Nothing Wrong with Having Needs—and Meeting Them

Isn't it funny how people-pleasers rush to meet the needs of others, yet dismiss their own? Isn't it strange how quick they are to take other people's judgment as gospel while assuming their own feelings, thoughts, and opinions are relatively worthless?

Perhaps you have a fear that *not* people-pleasing means you are irresponsible, selfish, or liable to get rejected or judged. Perhaps you feel that you are not as entitled to have your needs met as other people. Or perhaps, like many, you have the unconscious belief: "I only have worth if I am valuable to other people, if I please them, or if I make them happy." We'll explore all these beliefs in greater detail later in the book.

Occasionally, a people-pleaser will realize that something's got to give, and they may lash out, swing the other way, or suddenly be cold, harsh, and selfish. But this is not the solution, either. The problem is when you frame a situation as your needs VERSUS other people's needs. It is never either/or. It's never a competition for scarce resources.

You can have your needs met, **and** so can they.

A people-pleaser asks, "What can I do to get them to like me?" whereas a healthier mindset would have us ask, "So what if they don't like me?"

When you untangle yourself from other people's opinions and judgments, you free yourself to ask what YOU want, what you care about, and what you value. Then, you can act accordingly. When you "live on purpose" this way, you strengthen yourself. When you live an authentic and value-driven life, you're more courageous, so that when others disapprove, it genuinely does not matter. What could other people's opinions mean to you when you are following your heart and living the best life you know how?

You Are Not Omnipotent

Now, this may sound crazy, but here's a mind-blowing thought: people are living their own lives, which has nothing to do with you!

Jokes aside, a people-pleaser may make a continued error whenever they assume that other people's choices necessarily have something to do with them. Unconsciously, they put themselves at the center of everything. If someone was randomly rude to you, you automatically assume it's because of something you did. But really, isn't this a little arrogant?

Every person has their own life history, their own mindset, core beliefs, and hidden interior world. Some people don't even understand their own motivations, let alone make it clear to others why they do what they do! It may sound weird, but relax into the fact of your own probable insignificance in most people's lives.

You don't know what others are thinking and feeling, why they act, or what they want. You don't always have complete information about any situation and your role in it. So, that means you're off the hook and don't need to torture yourself with guesses and interpretations for other people's behaviors. "Why does my mother-in-law treat me this way? Does she do it on purpose? Maybe she thinks she's better than me. Have I possibly offended her?"

One possibility you may have overlooked: you have no idea what's going on in your mother-in-law's world, and in truth, she has barely given you a thought.

Remind yourself that **neutral is not negative.** Sometimes, people-pleasers can assume they've been rejected when all that's happened is . . . well, nothing. Most encounters and interactions are just neutral. And that's okay.

The "Separation of Tasks" Exercise

Enter the founder of individual psychology, psychiatrist Alfred Adler. His theories placed emphasis on the individual's need to adjust socially to his or her community. For him, feelings of harmonious belonging within a community were a big part of mental well-being. According to the authors of the book *The Courage to be Disliked*, Ichiro Kishimi and Fumitake Koga, **one of the most**

important things to master is the ability to ask, "Whose task is this?"

To explain what this means, consider the Separation of Tasks exercise. Speaking about Adler, the authors claim that, "All you can do with regard to your own life is choose the best path that you believe in. On the other hand, what kind of judgement do people pass on that choice? That is the task of other people and is not a matter you can do anything about."

There are things we have control over, and things we don't. Things we are responsible for, and things we aren't. Our "job" and others' jobs. The trick is to wisely discern the difference.

A people-pleaser may anxiously think, "I have to find a way to get this person to like me." But this task of liking someone or not—whose task is it? An alternative is to say, "It's up to *them* to decide if they like me or not." This is a much less anxiety-provoking thought and quite a revelation: Each person is ultimately responsible for their own opinions, reactions, and actions.

It may sound simple, but the ramifications of this short exercise can be profound. Whenever you are feeling distressed or confused, ask, "What is my task here?" With work colleagues, relationships, family members, or friends, pause and quickly ask if a certain task, idea, or thought is really your business. Is it your responsibility? Is it in your scope of control?

If not, let it go without guilt.

Chronic people-pleasers tend to take on everyone else's tasks. We make it our problem to ensure people like us. We take it upon ourselves to make sure everyone is happy, that there is no conflict, or that we are in their good books. And then we're anxious!

For example, you may tie yourself in knots trying to organize Christmas for your family. You have invited two people who are now feuding with one another, and you're anxiously wondering how to fix it, how to smooth over everyone's ruffled feathers, and how to make sure the rest of the family still has a nice time.

But you could instead pause and ask yourself to separate out their tasks from your own. You would see that:

- It is not your business what goes on between two other people.
- You cannot control how people respond to this feud or how they feel.
- Your only task is organizing Christmas to the best of your abilities (assuming this is a responsibility you were happy to take on in the first place! Was *that* your task...?).

Just asking the question, "What is MY task here?" can save you mountains of people-pleasing behavior and anxiety. When you catch yourself fretting over what others think or feel, pause again to remind yourself that is not your job. The Serenity Prayer is great for people-pleasers since we need to remember the difference between what we can control and what we can't. **"Grant me the serenity to accept the things I cannot change, the courage to change the things I cannot accept, and the wisdom to know the difference."**

In truth, you *can* fret over other people's tasks if you really want to. But why would you want to when it doesn't help them and certainly doesn't help you?

Chapter 2: Are You Generous? Or Just Afraid of Rejection?

Some of us engage in people-pleasing because we desperately want other people's approval, validation, and liking. But sometimes, people-pleasing can come from a slightly different place. **"Rejection sensitivity" is what it sounds like—the heightened and unreasonable fear of someone rejecting you**. More commonly, though, the real problem is all the stuff we do to *avoid* that perceived potential for rejection. **One big way we can attempt to avoid the horror of being rejected is to engage in people-pleasing.**

Many people-pleasers feel awful at the prospect that they should be less kind, less generous, or less forgiving. But consider this:

Is your motivation *really* compassion and kindness? Or is it sometimes an attempt, conscious or unconscious, to try to control people? If you view things this way, then you quickly realize that letting go of rejection, fears, and people-pleasing behaviors is precisely what will allow you to be *more* generous—or, more genuinely generous!

Being giving is a beautiful thing. But it's less beautiful when it's purely a strategy to help us moderate anxiety. A study in the 2016 academic journal *Frontiers in Human Neuroscience* (Dominguez et al.) found that "agreeable" people had a tendency to people-please in order to avoid social stress. The researchers discovered, using fMRI scans, that when faced with an opportunity to say no, areas of the brain associated with cognitive dissonance lit up. However, when they said yes, those same areas went offline.

What this suggests is that saying yes to requests is a way to reduce inner stress and uneasiness (some might call it guilt!). The authors had actually uncovered the physiological basis for that feeling of "I just can't say no!" The fear of rejection causes us distress, but by saying yes, we quell that anxiety. So, being generous and giving is not really about the other person at all—it's about regulating *ourselves*.

Of course, this doesn't always work out so well because by saying yes, we open ourselves to being taken advantage of, to agreeing to things that actually violate our own boundaries, and to making our own feelings of calm *dependent on us being generous and useful to others*. So, what happens when we really do need to say no?

Fearing rejection, we may fail to set limits and boundaries, and we seem to get stuck in one-sided relationships with people who take and take. But once we're in these situations, we may feel even less able to say no—in other words, the anxiety about being rejected actually increases. For example, you've agreed to look after your friend's dog even though you really don't have the time. You said yes just to keep the peace and avoid awkwardness...

But now he's asked you to look after the dog again. And he keeps asking. The pressure to say yes is even greater now (you've set a precedent, haven't you?), so you keep saying yes. Before you know it, you're trapped in a sickening and reinforcing cycle of guilt and obligation. Perhaps in all this, your own dog sits at home, missing out on her walks while you're away, which makes you feel awful. You give and give and give, and yet you have low self-worth, you're stressed, and you're resentful. In comparison, the prospect of being rejected by your friend if you had said no suddenly doesn't seem so bad!

Rejection sensitivity is more common than you'd think . . . and the irony is that it often has the opposite of the intended effect. For example:

- You're terrified of being rejected in a big job interview, but this makes you behave in meek, unconfident ways during that interview, causing the interviewers to pass you over for someone with more faith in themselves.
- Meeting new people, your desperate need to impress causes you to hog the conversation and be boastful. They're not impressed.
- In dating, your fear of rejection may lead you to waste time with people you don't actually like. By doing whatever you can to avoid *them* rejecting *you*, you miss out on a

crucial detail: you're not keen on them yourself!

How to Break the Fear of Rejection Cycle

Rejection is a normal part of life. The weird things we do to avoid rejection, however, can be far from normal!

In their bid to be accepted by others, people-pleasers can be timid, neurotic, and inauthentic. Worse still, others may perceive them as false, passive aggressive, or even manipulative, creating a self-fulfilling prophesy where people actually may feel pushed to reject them.

The good news is that this is all fixable. No, we cannot avoid rejection, and there is no way to magically make everyone accept and embrace us. But we can make sure that we don't let the sting of rejection spiral out of control and hurt more than it needs to.

Travis Corigan created the *Rejection Inoculation Program*, and his strategy is not to twist you out of shape so nobody ever rejects you again. Rather, it's to *make* sure that the next time you are rejected (and it *will* happen), you are resilient against it, and *though* it may hurt, it doesn't shake your self-worth to its core.

Corigan's technique is a form of what psychologists call exposure therapy. You repeatedly expose yourself to the feared stimulus, but in a safe environment that you control. Why go through all this torture? Because you are undoing a **core belief at the root of people-pleasing behavior: I cannot survive rejection. I must avoid it at all costs.**

The thing is, this belief is actually not true. You *can* survive it, and the only way to prove this to yourself is to willingly experience rejection and notice how you feel. Corigan's program has three easy steps:

1. Set yourself a quota
2. Set a time domain
3. Make attempts to hit that quota

What's a quota? It's simply the number of times you are rejected. Yup—you are deliberately seeking out rejection. Merely framing rejection as something that you ask for and are in control of takes some of its power away. See the whole exercise as a game or challenge, and not some life-or-death agony.

"By turning the thing you most want to avoid into the key performance indicator (KPI) that you should optimize is a righteous trick for your brain. You utilize one part of your motivation centers to break this log jam between two competing motivations you have: the life you want for yourself and your primate programming that being rejected from the tribe means death," says Corigan.

The approach may sound terrifying, but it's a brilliant way to completely turn your mindset upside down. If you run screaming from rejection, you may think it's a triumph when you don't have to experience it. On the other hand, never experiencing it allows you to fear it all the more. Rejection becomes a big, terrifying black hole in your psyche, and when you eventually do encounter it (because, again, you will!), you are unprepared and in the worst possible position to cope with it.

When you "inoculate yourself" against rejection and actually *rehearse* the process, you realize something. **Rejection is not that**

big a deal. That queasy feeling in the pit of your stomach, that awful hot feeling on your face, and that sinking sense of dread and self-loathing . . . it's all transient. Who cares? Open your eyes and look around—you're still alive, you're still a worthy human being, and the world didn't end. And what's more, there may be a new stirring inside you, something a little like confidence.

Let's look at an example of the inoculation program in the context of being overly generous and not saying no.

Katie is the biggest martyr you'll ever meet. She's a teacher's assistant who regularly buys things for her students from her own pocket and stays late after school to help struggling kids. She volunteers for more organizations and charities than she can count. She tirelessly dedicates most of her weekends to organizing community events and babysitting her nieces and nephews, or helping her elderly mother with errands.

She does all this because she's a good, kind person. She also does it because she's terrified that if she says no, all these people will angrily abandon her. As you can imagine, Katie has extremely low self-worth that is entirely conditional on how much she does for others. She's frequently exhausted and stressed out, but at least all this work proves her value and prevents others from rejecting her, right?

She tried out a version of Corigan's program, and it looked like this:

Quota: start by politely saying no to a request I don't have time for, and not budging no matter how guilty I feel or am made to feel

Do this at least once a week to start, just to test it out. Increase frequency later on.

Katie comes down with the flu. The school has let her take some time off, but Katie's mother sees this as an opportunity to ask Katie to come over to her house and help her clean out her basement, "Since you're free." Katie takes a deep breath, and says, "I'm feeling pretty exhausted, Mom. I think it's a no from me." Then she waits. She doesn't apologize, she doesn't beg forgiveness, and she doesn't immediately leap in with an alternative suggestion to soften her no.

Are you wondering what happens next? Well, the truth is that Katie's mother's response is not all that relevant. Katie has already decided that she will say no and stick to it *no matter what response she gets.* That's because she is acting for herself and not for some desired response from others. She is untangling herself from people-pleasing and reconnecting with the idea of pleasing herself.

In a later chapter, we'll look more closely at boundary setting and how to say no assertively yet with kindness. But for now, like Katie, the idea is simply to become proactive and deliberately seek rejection on your own terms. Katie's mother doesn't in fact disown her, even if she's a little surprised. The next week, Katie says no when the school demands she organizes the bake sale. She notices that the more she says no, the easier it becomes because of three important insights:

1. The rejection she assumed was coming didn't in fact come, and
2. If it did come, it wasn't as bad as she predicted it would be, and
3. If it was that bad, she realized that she was more than able to cope with it!

Over the course of a few months, Katie challenges the core belief that **I cannot survive rejection. I must avoid it at all costs.** She replaces it with new ones. *Rejection is not the end of the world. I am a good person even if I say no, and even if someone rejects me for it. I can cope with people being unhappy with me.*

How you set your quota, what your quota is, and what time frame you choose is up to you. You could decide you want to make one cold call a day at work and count the times people turn down your pitch. You could aim to talk to a new person every three days. You could commit to reaching out to romantic interests, or take the risk of inviting relatively new friends to meet up and get to know each other better. The big difference is that you are not running away from rejection but encountering it in a controlled, deliberate fashion.

Here are a few things to keep in mind as you try Corigan's approach:

Have Self-Compassion

Think of someone you love, and now imagine them experiencing the pain of rejection.

Do you feel like laughing and jeering at them, or think that they're losers? Do you feel like saying, "Don't be such a baby," or, "Maybe they're right to reject you"?

Chances are, you just feel kind, tender compassion. You want to hug them and say, "Don't worry, it doesn't matter. I still think you're awesome!"

Try to see if you can have that very same reaction to yourself when you experience rejection. Acknowledge that it hurts. Not just for you but for every human being. It's okay to feel bad about it. At the same time, you accept both yourself and the emotions you're feeling. Rejection is hard enough without feeling bad about feeling bad!

Challenge Your Narratives

Let's say you never ask anyone out because you're afraid of them rejecting you. The story you tell yourself is, "If I ask people out, they'll be offended and annoyed, and they may even be rude or insulting to me." So you don't ask anyone out, but this means that you never get to test the truth of this narrative.

If you deliberately seek out rejection, though, you discover that this story is pretty inaccurate. People may well reject you, but instead their response is to be flattered and surprised and to kindly and politely say no, letting you know they still appreciate the effort. Unless you test out your narrative, though, you never give yourself the chance to correct it.

You *think* you are sparing yourself some pain by clinging to the old narrative. But what about the pain of forever believing such a story? What about the low self-esteem it brings, the distrust of others, the pessimism? What about all the opportunities that you miss because you believe that story?

Focus on Process and Not Outcome

Who is in control of your world?
What determines your state of mind?

For people-pleasers, their sense of worth always seems to rest outside of themselves. They give that power to others. If *they* think you're good, then you're good. If *they* think you're bad, then that's what you are.

Furthermore, a people-pleaser always cares about the outcome. Will they approve? What will they say? What should you do to ensure the "right" outcome?

But this "external locus of control" and a focus on outcome saps the joy out of life and makes you feel powerless. To counter it, focus instead on the process, not on the outcome. For example, with Corigan's exercise, you make progress every time you act to fill your quota. That is something you are in control of. Your quota is not to elicit any particular response from anyone else—it's only about you and your actions.

Give yourself credit for trying, and forget about what other people think of those attempts or what comes of them. The process of challenging limiting beliefs, of facing your fear—this is where the value lies no matter what the result is!

Chapter 3: "Fawning"—A Response to Trauma

Picture a couple having an argument. Voices are raised and things are getting heated. Then, all of a sudden, Person A starts smiling sweetly. "Look, let's just forget this whole thing, okay? It's all so silly; it doesn't matter. You're right about everything. Can I make you some cocoa? With marshmallows? What else would you like?" Person B is confused, wondering where all the hugs and kisses are coming from and what happened to the argument they were having only seconds ago.

Person B has witnessed what is called the **"fawning response." In the face of trauma**

and conflict, some people respond with anger, some respond by fleeing . . . and some, like Person A, respond with a flood of appeasing, soothing, and conciliatory behavior. "Fight or flight" is an option for some people, but for those with a history of trauma, another option when faced with threat is to go into fawning mode and try to make it all better.

Picture an animal defensively rolling onto its back, trying to appear as meek and agreeable as possible so that it's spared by a powerful predator. Fawning is an attempt to fly under the radar rather than engage in conflict. It's a way of deflecting attention.

In a crisis or disagreement, is your first instinct to soothe, calm, or please others?

Do you do anything to avoid conflict—even if that means ignoring your own needs?

In a stressful interaction, is your focus on other people's emotions?

Fawning behavior is actually a kind of trauma response. This behavior, in other words, is something you might have learned in childhood, where "rolling over" this way was the only thing that helped you survive conflict. Some people may also find that their fawning behavior accompanies the tendency to freeze during conflict. Maybe your mind goes blank, your heart races, and you dissociate. You are the proverbial "deer in headlights."

At the core of this fawning and freezing behavior is the unconscious core belief: **"the price for peace with others is compliance. If I make other people happy, then I will be safe."** The mindset is one where safety is all that matters, and your goal is to do whatever it takes to achieve that safety.

Michael had an abusive father growing up. His father would get angry, yell, and break things around the home, going on rampages that would terrify the family. Early on, as a young and defenseless child, Michael learned that the best strategy was to do whatever it took to appease his father's anger.

This meant agreeing with everything he said, quickly complying with any requests, and generally making himself as small and non-threatening as possible. After all, if he made one wrong move, his father would interpret it as a threat, and then more abuse would follow. Michael became so good at this strategy that he even learned to pre-empt his father's moods, walking on eggshells and finding ways to manage his strong emotions on his father's behalf.

Here is the sad thing: this approach genuinely did work for Michael. It *did* prevent conflict and keep him safe. But in adulthood, Michael realized what this safety cost him. Those who use fawning behavior are often confused about their own boundaries, unable to meet their own needs, and, ironically, vulnerable to more abuse.

Not all people-pleasers are doing so as a part of a fawning response, but if this is the case for you, know that there are ways to heal and rewrite the narrative for yourself. Your task will be to change the core belief that **compliance = safety**. Those with abusive backgrounds may also strike another unconscious bargain: "If I attach myself to this powerful person and make them need and like me, then I can win favor and be safe." But that powerful person may well be the same person who is creating the lack of safety in the first place! It's not unlike Stockholm Syndrome, where hostages attempt to control an abusive dynamic by bonding with their captor.

People who default to fawning behavior would sooner absorb any emotional blow than speak up, say no, and face the fallout. Unfortunately, knowing how to erect and assert healthy boundaries is a part of being a mature adult. How do we get out of this bind?

Get Professional Help

PTSD (post-traumatic stress disorder) is seldom something that people can deal with on their own. A mental health professional, however, can point you in the direction of evidence-based therapies that can help you rewire both your body and mind, and untangle the learned trauma response. Consider EMDR therapy, medication, and talk therapy—or a combination of all three.

Reparent Yourself

Today's dysfunction was yesterday's coping mechanism.

Dr. Arielle Schwatz is a C-PTSD (complex PTSD) expert and explains that abusive or dysfunctional parenting can create children who are hyper-focused on their parents' emotions. To survive an unhealthy home environment, these children felt compelled to take care of their parents' emotional needs. To do this, they needed to suppress their needs. They also needed to put their authentic selves and their feelings on the back burner. These feelings are still there, however, and may show up in adulthood as the tendency to recreate these same "enmeshed" or codependent relationships (more on codependency in a later chapter). Cut off from their own needs, such people may feel numb, dissociated, and inauthentic.

The insight of "inner child work" and re-parenting yourself is that **we are able to give ourselves today what we did not receive as children**. In the past, we had to adapt in certain ways to survive less-than-ideal childhoods, but now, as adults, we have a choice. We can rewrite the core belief of "To be safe, I must comply" to "I am allowed to be who I am. I am a good person. It is safe to have needs and to ask for them to be met."

Overcoming a difficult childhood takes time, but it can be done:

- Set boundaries. Have limits and defend those limits (more on this in Chapter 6).
- Stop explaining yourself or justifying your choices. You don't owe that to people.
- Allow someone else to do the work for a change. Delegate or ask for help instead of doing it all yourself.
- Promise not to abandon your inner child. Decide that your priority will be to protect and defend them, rather than to serve the interests of bullies or those who trample on your boundaries.
- Be your own mother (give yourself unconditional compassion and love) and your own father (protect yourself with solid boundaries—and defend them!).

Reconnect with Your Principles and Values

Fawners have substituted their own judgment with the needs and demands of others. But you strengthen and orient yourself when you remind yourself of what's important to **you**, and why. It may take time to clarify your authentic self, find out what you truly want in life, not to mention find the courage to express it. But you may also find that speaking up is itself something that gives you courage. For fawners, it can be scary to be "seen." But in small ways, you can challenge yourself to speak up and express your genuine opinion, even if it goes against other peoples' opinions or causes a little friction.

People who have learned to fawn over others are unaware of their secret superpower: that they have the ability to **create safety for themselves**. That they can be safe in their own convictions. They do not have to strike a deal with anyone to feel safe, but can feel safe right now.

Become an Expert on Your Own Feelings

Fawners are experts at other people's feelings. They may be so tuned into other peoples' needs that they seem psychic at times. However, what they're not good at is knowing how *they* feel.

If you're a people-pleasing fawner, you may have learned early in life to turn your emotions off. What good would that do, anyway, since there's no chance of them being heard or respected, right? But by dissociating, you sever your mind-body connection and lose touch with who you are on a very deep level. You may even find yourself feeling lost and vague—who are *you* amidst all these other people and their desires and demands?

There are plenty of ways to reconnect with your genuine feelings and to slowly teach yourself that **it is safe to feel**:

- Try body-mind strengthening activities like dance or yoga. Drop any expectations or "shoulds" about how to move your body, and listen to how it wants to move.
- "Befriend" the emotions that emerge in you, whatever they are. Literally picture your feelings as people sitting around a table. Welcome them all and ask them what they have to say. Your

feelings were not heard as a child, but you can listen to them now as an adult.
- Prick your ears and watch out for feelings of guilt—the signature emotion of the fawn response. Try the "separation of tasks" exercise above and consciously choose to let go of things that are not your responsibility and not under your control.

Have Fun!

One amazing way to gently shift the tendency to fawn over others is to encourage the opposite mindset, i.e., one that is playful, carefree, and creative. As a child, you were meant to be loved and kept safe so that you could enjoy yourself, grow, and explore the world. That sense of play and exploration was cut short with a premature feeling of responsibility for others. You may have developed the opinion that having fun was too risky, and that it may actually be dangerous to relax your vigilance for even a second. It's all very serious!

But right now, you can reconnect with that sense of innocence that you may have missed out on. Take your inner child out on a "playdate" and ask them what they really want to do. No, it doesn't have to make sense, and no, nobody else's opinion matters.

Maybe you buy yourself some silly craft supplies or go for a walk without any idea of where you'll go. Maybe you just enjoy having a free afternoon without any plan at all and zero idea of what you're "supposed to do." If it's fun and it makes you happy, why not?

Chapter 4: Why Conflict Avoidance is Actually a High-Risk Strategy

So far, we have considered a few answers to the question, what causes people-pleasing?

- The need to be liked
- The fear of rejection
- The desire to stay safe

Let's consider one more cause of people-pleasing behavior: the need to avoid conflict. Here, "conflict" means disagreement, upsetting others, awkwardness, friction, misunderstanding, or just bad vibes in general.

You do not have to have grown up in an abusive home to want to desperately avoid conflict. But you may nevertheless have internalized the lesson that not giving people what they want usually results in bad outcomes, and it's easier just to be "nice" and avoid rocking the boat.

We've all done this at some point or other, whether it's biting our tongue when we really wanted to speak out or pretending to go along with something just because the alternative seemed like too much to deal with.

Again, there's nothing wrong with trying to avoid conflict, and there's nothing intrinsically valuable about disagreeing! The challenge for people-pleasers is simply to find the right balance. Being a mediator who values harmony and cohesion is a great thing, and you can be proud of that if it's a skill you have. Being terrified of disagreement or inevitable bad feelings, on the other hand, is a problem.

Conflict avoidance is where we avoid conflict at all costs. It is *not* the same as being easy-going, accommodating, or able to find mutual resolutions to problems. Conflict avoidance is where we carefully weigh up everyone's needs and find a solution that makes everyone happy—except we completely ignore ourselves in that equation. That's why, in fact, this strategy itself may become the problem.

Here are some examples of conflict avoidance as a people-pleasing strategy:

You quickly change the topic when someone says something wrong or offensive, just to avoid calling them out or causing an argument.

You put up with uncomfortable situations rather than kick up a fuss. You don't want to offend!

You go silent or flee interactions rather than disagree or face awkwardness.

You deny problems or how you feel about them. You'd rather swallow your own discomfort than cause it in someone else.

You don't express yourself honestly in case it makes waves.

You agree to unreasonable demands to keep the peace . . . but then grow resentful about it anyway.

As with all forms of people-pleasing we've explored, **conflict avoidance costs you something enormous: your authenticity.** Honest communication and genuine intimacy fly out the window. Problems fester beneath the surface, and people are completely in the dark about how everyone truly feels. Most commonly, it's not conflict avoidance so much as conflict deferral—the problem often comes back to bite you later on!

The Terrible Tale of the "Gunnysack"

"Gunnysacking" is a sure sign of conflict avoidance and people-pleasing. This is how the tale of the gunnysack usually plays out:

Melissa is the most junior member of her team at work, and a good decade younger than everyone else. Because she has low self-esteem and she's petrified of causing a scene and potentially losing her job, she quietly puts up with behavior she really dislikes. She smiles and complies when asked to clean the office or fetch coffee, even though it's not in her job description. She keeps quiet when people steal her ideas and flaunt them as their own. She says nothing when her boss repeatedly misspells her name.

What Melissa is doing is quietly accumulating each of these little insults and injuries into a gunnysack. She holds on to every one of them, and the sack grows bigger and bigger. One day, the receptionist is a little curt with her, and Melissa tries to put that, too, into the gunnysack. Except by now it's so full that it suddenly explodes. All at once, Melissa loses her temper and lashes out at the receptionist, who is completely bewildered, and Melissa is in fact disciplined later for her outburst.

The gunnysack tale is a tale of irony—in wanting to avoid conflict at all costs, you actually wind up with one big, catastrophic conflict at the end, when you cannot take any more. Even worse, after the flood, you may feel so guilty and horrible that you double down on your future efforts to "be nice" and never, ever let anyone down again . . .

Out comes a new gunnysack.

But . . . What's the Alternative?

People-pleasers can feel genuinely mystified about how to fix conflict avoidance since they can't imagine what a healthy alternative looks like. Be more argumentative? Happily embrace conflict?

The first thing to realize is that pretending to be cool with things you aren't cool with doesn't actually change the problem. The situation may *appear* okay, but that is only on the surface and usually only temporary. The truth is that disagreements, grievances, problems, and issues all continue to exist, and pretending they don't doesn't change a thing besides maybe delaying the inevitable.

Unless you **consciously address conflict**, you only create misunderstanding, disappointment, or a nice full gunnysack waiting to burst. And you get all that on top of the original problem you were trying to run away from in the first place.

Here are some ways to consciously address conflict rather than store it away where it can earn compound interest! It's not as difficult as it may seem at first.

Use AND Not BUT

If you hate being contrary or disagreeing with others, then try doing it without using the word "but." It's a simple trick that teaches you that two people can in fact have different viewpoints at the same time without them necessarily threatening one another. For example, just because you feel right, it doesn't mean the other person is automatically wrong. You can both be right! Express this by saying "and" instead of "but."

For example, "I know that you're keen on a vacation soon, *and* I'm aware that we may need to watch our savings if we want to reach our goal this month." (You express your opinion without positioning it against theirs. Look how nicely they both sit together in the sentence without bothering one another!)

Try a Hypothetical

People-pleasers can sometimes think that to be assertive, they need to loudly and boldly claim their opinion, everyone else be damned. But you don't have to. You can introduce a difference of opinion in the form of a question or a suggestion to consider some alternative scenario.

For example, "A vacation would be amazing right now, I agree. Is there a way we can organize one while still meeting our savings goals for this month?"

Draw Attention to the Impact of Actions

It can feel awkward to draw attention to your disagreement or conflicting opinion, especially in a work context, because it can come across as an emotional or psychological admission. It can seem like all you're doing is presenting the other person with the fact of your disagreement, which can sometimes feel like a dead end or even a challenge. But you don't have to frame things this way.

Keep your focus on the practical real-world outcomes of different ideas, opinions, or actions. For example, "If we go on a vacation next month, it'll probably cost us around $xxx. How is that going to impact our savings plan?"

Become Curious About the Deeper Causes

Is there an underlying issue that it would be wise to address directly? If you disagree with someone, sometimes the issue is completely resolved when you dig a little deeper and find out the cause of that disagreement. If you do this, you get the chance to resolve things some other way.

For example, "I thought we both agreed on our savings goals, but it seems like a vacation is more of a priority for you now. I'm curious, what's changed?"

In this example, you may discover that the vacation is actually an attempt to solve a deeper problem, let's say work stress. Once you know what this problem is, you can solve it directly, maybe without spending money on a vacation—it's a win-win situation.

You'll notice that in all of the above strategies, expressing a different opinion does not require you to be forceful, inconsiderate, pushy, or arrogant. In a very real way, this is the *real* path to avoiding conflict!

With good communication, reasonable boundaries, and a spirit of open-mindedness, you approach any difference of opinion calmly and without seeing it as a threat. And that gives you the best possible chances of *resolving* conflict, not just sweeping it under the carpet to be uncovered later.

If conflict avoidance is a stubborn issue for you, it may be worth working on your core assumptions on your own time before you encounter potential conflict with others. Here are a few things to guide your process:

What are you really avoiding?

The superficial answer is "conflict!" but ask yourself what you are actually avoiding by avoiding conflict. Does it have something to do with the need to be liked, the need to prevent rejection, or the need to maintain harmony as a matter of self-preservation? It may be a special blend of all of these!

Use the "Five Whys" technique and keep burrowing down to what you are really running away from. For example:

I don't want to keep paying so much money to be a bridesmaid several times a year, and I hate the stress of it all, but I never say no.

Why?

I don't want to get into a big argument about it. If I say no, then my friends will be upset with me.

Why?

Because they'll think that I'm a bad friend.

Why?

Because good friends do whatever they're told, no question.

Why?

Because if they don't, then why would people want them around?

Why?

Because people only have value if they are useful to others. If they aren't, then there's no reason for them not to be discarded!

And there it is. You are not really afraid of conflict, but of being discarded or abandoned if you don't comply. The conflict is a scary thing to avoid only because it would lead to this discarding, which is what you're really afraid of.

The thing about this technique is that you may be surprised by what you uncover, and your deepest, most hidden motivations are always going to be completely unique to you. Notice in the above example that the answers to the questions aren't necessarily true. They are simply a reflection of the core beliefs, assumptions, and narratives that are being held. It may be that once you clearly verbalize these hidden assumptions, they have less of a hold on you. "Wow. Is this really how I want to feel about my friends?"

This exercise could lead you to more thoughtfully consider **the cost of conflict avoidance.**

Trying to avoid conflict is a strategy purely designed to reduce harm, but you may realize that it doesn't actually do this, and in fact, it creates additional harms of its own.

You lose self-respect, you trash your own boundaries and invite others to do the same, you quietly hold on to resentments, and perhaps worst of all, you forego the opportunity to have a genuine and intimate connection with another person.

Conflict may be unpleasant, but it is real. And it's also the only thing that, by going through it, allows us to access positive outcomes like forgiveness, reconciliation, and deeper understanding. Isn't that worth more than the illusion of peace?

Takeaways

- People-pleasing is a complex learned behavior, but it can be understood and changed. One of the most common underlying causes is the need to be liked.
- We can counter this mindset by remembering we are like inkblots (i.e., what people see is about them, not about you) and understanding that your worth does not come from other people's approval.
- When you untangle yourself from other people's opinions and judgments, you free yourself to ask what YOU want, what

you care about, and what you value. The "separation of tasks" exercise helps you to tease apart your responsibilities from other peoples'—their feelings are not your business.
- Over-giving stemming from fear of rejection is not genuine generosity. Break the cycle by changing the core belief: "I cannot survive rejection." Instead, court rejection deliberately and teach yourself that it doesn't define you. Challenge your narratives with self-compassion, and focus on process, not outcome.
- People-pleasing is sometimes part of a bigger behavioral response to childhood trauma called "fawning," i.e., a flood of appeasing, soothing, and conciliatory behavior.
- You may need professional help to address a fawning habit, but you can also make strides by re-parenting yourself. This entails choosing to give to yourself now what you weren't given as a child. Reparenting also entails connecting with your values and principles, getting in tune with your own emotions, and learning to have fun!
- People-pleasers can be conflict avoidant, but this is actually a high-risk strategy, and you may gather resentments only to

explode later ("gunnysacking"). Instead, use "and" instead of "but" in conversations, or try the "Five Whys" technique to get to the heart of what you're really avoiding.

Part 2: The People-Pleaser's Survival Kit

Chapter 5: Six Different Ways to Say NO

For habitual people-pleasers, saying no can seem impossible. It doesn't matter if we've just been asked to break the laws of physics or be in two places at one time—if someone asks, we find ourselves saying "yes" and hoping we'll figure something out.

In the last section, we considered all the deep roots of people-pleasing, but whatever your reason for doing it, rest assured that you can unlearn this behavior and do something different. Saying no is something that we can learn to do even if we're not one hundred percent confident, and even if we don't feel truly assertive yet.

This chapter will work at expanding your "no" vocabulary—because there's a no for every occasion!

Trevor Powell is a psychologist and assertiveness expert who has outlined six different ways to politely but assertively turn down a request.

Direct NO

This means what it sounds like: You simply say "no." You don't follow up with an apology, explanation, or justification. You don't ask permission to say no or immediately launch into conciliatory behavior to make up for your refusal. Your no just stands there on its own, strong and bold. Think of it this way: the less you add to this brave and noble no, the stronger it is.

Use a direct no when someone has violated a boundary, especially if it's not the first time. It's also good for outrageous or disrespectful requests. "You want me to do your homework for you? Uh, no."

Reasoned NO

Take note, this is a no with a reason, not an excuse. The reason is there to help the other person understand why you are saying no; it's not to exonerate you or open up room for negotiations. It's always perfectly okay to say no even if you don't have a reason or don't want to share it. But giving a reason is a courteous thing to do.

The only trick is to keep it brief and sincere. Again, the more you add, the less legitimate it will seem.

"I'm sorry I can't come; I'll be at my grandmother's birthday party that weekend."

Reflecting NO

This is more polite still because you acknowledge and reflect the asker's feelings and situation.

"I know it would be easier for you if I helped out, but I can't this time."

This way, you are noticing and reflecting the other person's experience ... without letting it undermine your own boundary or dilute your "no." It's a good idea to remember to omit the word "but." Simply follow up your acknowledgement of their feelings with your polite refusal, without making it seem as though these two things clash. Just remember that people tend to mentally erase everything that was said immediately before the word "but."

"I know you're upset. I can't make it."

Raincheck NO

You're not saying no forever and ever. You're just saying no right now. In the future, you may say yes. Your friend needs your help to move into their new apartment, but your mom has just died and you can't imagine facing anyone right now. You say no because you can't right now, but you do want to keep the door open for when your friend needs you in the future.

"I'm sorry, I can't do it. I can come over in a few weeks' time, if you like, and help you unpack?"

Of course, if you're an expert people-pleaser, you'll have to remain vigilant and stop yourself from making a promise you don't want to or cannot keep later on.

A variation on this is to simply not give an answer right away, i.e., put a raincheck on your response itself. Say something like, "Oh, I'm not sure. Can I get back to you on that?" or, "Let me just confirm with my calendar/spouse/work colleagues and let you know." This gives you some time to gather yourself and decide if it's a request you want to comply with or not.

Enquiring NO

Much like the raincheck no, an enquiring no is all about communicating the *spirit* of compliance and helpfulness, even though the exact request in that moment cannot be met. Be warm and friendly and keep dialogue open so you can both find an alternative.

"I'm booked with clients for the next three weeks. Maybe I can refer you to a friend of mine?"

You could keep it even more open-ended than that and simply use a few questions to show that you are listening and do care. The trick is that you still say no, but the other person feels at least that you explored the options with them.

"Are you available for a photo shoot on the 26th?"
"Hmm, unfortunately I'm booked with clients for the next three weeks. What kind of shoot were you looking for?"
"Just an hour-long portrait session. I could come into the studio."
"Hmm. It is just you?"
"Well, me and my wife."
"I see. Well, if you give me your number, I can call you if I get any cancellations, but I'm afraid I can't fit you in right now."
"Oh well. Thanks, anyway!"

Broken Record NO

Sometimes you'll encounter someone who views your boundary as a personal challenge. They'll keep pushing and pushing. Your best response when this happens? Keep pushing back.

The broken record technique is simply when you calmly repeat your refusal without really adding anything and without getting distracted by tangents and diversions. You imagine yourself as a boring, flat surface that can only ever give the same answer. Eventually, the other person has no choice but to accept it. The key here, though, is not to get dragged into any pleading or negotiating. If you don't give the other person any threads to pursue, they have no choice but to drop the request eventually.

"So, can you come get me from the airport?"
"Sorry, I don't think I can. I have my exam."
"Yeah, but can't you come and get me *before* your exam?"
"No, I'll need to focus on the exam that day."
"Really? The whole day? It's not such a big deal. The airport's only forty-five minutes from your house . . ."
"Sorry, no. That day I'm dedicating to the exam I have."
"Wow, seems kind of mean."
"Like I said, I've got to do that exam, so I can't help you."
"Okay, fine."

Notice how the person saying no never takes any bait or gets tangled in details, which would only end up with their boundary being eroded until they basically said yes. They also don't respond when the other person makes an emotional appeal ("You're mean!") and keeps on with that broken record. It's not a pleasant conversation, but it's far better than the alternative!

The above techniques look pretty simple, and that's because they are. But they may nevertheless take some presence of mind to remember in the heat of the moment. Here are a few tips to help you become a master at saying no:

- Rehearse it. It's a little cheesy, but it'll give you confidence and courage. If you have a trusted friend, rehearse it with them.
- Don't over explain, justify yourself, or ask for permission. Your body language and tone of voice can also communicate a lot to the other person, so be mindful and speak clearly, calmly, and confidently. Don't say no while your body language is saying maybe.
- If appropriate, say no by email or text. It's easier and gives you time.
- Don't try to compensate for your no. Even if you feel guilty, it's not your responsibility to try to solve the other person's problem for them, help them manage their emotional response to your boundary, or repent for that

boundary in some way. You don't owe them just because you said no!

With practice, turning down requests gets easier and easier. People may be a bit surprised if you've always been a classic doormat—you may even surprise yourself!—but prepare for the fact that they may also treat you with a lot more care and consideration going forward. A people-pleaser's worst fear is that others are out there angry or disappointed in them, but in reality, a person who calmly and confidently takes charge of their own limits and needs inspires trust and respect in others.

Finding it hard to say no is a manifestation of a certain mindset. It's a reflection of our beliefs about ourselves, others, and the world. We can change our behavior and gradually change the way we think, or we can change the way we think and allow that to change how we behave. Your best bet is to try to do both!

Challenging the Beliefs that Stop You from Saying No

Ask yourself, what are your beliefs about this tiny but powerful word *no*? Some people would say:

- It's rude to turn down a request (or mean, unkind, or even ill-mannered)
- Saying no means you're a selfish person who lacks compassion
- If you don't do what people ask, you'll upset them
- Unless you say yes to every request, you're not entitled to ask for help yourself

Can you add any of your own? These beliefs, however, are totally unhelpful, and that's because they're just not true. When you believe some version of the above, your conclusion is that you can never say no. But then that means that you agree to things that undermine your values and cross your boundaries, and you may deplete your resources, whether that's time, energy, or money.

People who have a healthy relationship with the word *no* think differently. They believe that:

- I'm not rejecting the person; I'm just saying no to this particular request
- I have limited resources, and so I have to prioritize; I cannot say yes to everything
- Every "yes" to something is automatically a "no" to something else
- Saying no is not personal
- I am entitled to have limits and desires and to communicate these
- Everyone has the right to ask, and everyone has the right to decline

If you catch yourself trying to mentally "explain" why you absolutely cannot say no to a request, pause and see if your justifications hold any water. Try to replace them with a healthier alternative above and see if reframing things makes you feel differently.

Chapter 6: Everyone Needs Boundaries... Including You!

When you people-please, you often deny your own needs. You take the hit and quietly resent it, or bite your tongue when you desperately need to speak up. Poor boundaries dent your self-esteem, weaken your genuine connections to others, and sometimes force you to try to meet your needs indirectly, with bad results.

If all of this is true, then why do people continue to have poor boundaries and choose people-pleasing instead?

The reason is because there are benefits to being a people-pleaser. It actually does pay off—at least in the short term. In the moment, you may feel popular and in demand. People may approve of you, and you may even get the addictive ego-stroking that comes with people openly acknowledging that you are sacrificing yourself.

"Oh, you're a saint! Thank you so much. I don't know what I'd do without you!"
"He's such a great guy. He'd give you the shirt off his back."
"You're my star employee. You're ultra-productive and nothing is ever too much trouble."

This high is momentary, though. What's more, it's usually quite superficial—i.e., the approval you garner seems to rest entirely and exclusively on your doing what others wanted. How genuine could someone's approval and respect have really been if it shatters the moment you dare to have your own opinion, limits, or priorities?

If you're the kind of person who has derived much of their self-identity from being nice, kind, accommodating, and charitable, this role can be hard to give up. That's why you need to remind yourself of how expensive it is; i.e., what it costs you: your self-esteem, your sense of calm and balance, your dignity, your time and resources, and the opportunity to pursue your own life on your own terms according to your own values.

That's a big price to pay!

People-pleasing has some benefits, but it has far, far more drawbacks.

Setting appropriate boundaries is an adult life skill that everyone needs to master. Many people-pleasers unconsciously think, "Oh, setting boundaries is something other people do . . ." and they create a special exception for themselves. But it doesn't matter if you're a busy parent or an employee in a high-powered career . . . everyone needs boundaries, including you.

Before we look at how to set and maintain boundaries, let's consider a few deeper core beliefs that may be standing in the way. You may say, "Oh, I couldn't take a day off. The place would be a circus without me," but deep down, your reason for not setting boundaries at work is not really because you are needed. Beneath this excuse may be beliefs like:

I don't deserve to get what I want or need.

My needs aren't that important, or not as important as other people's.
Having boundaries shows I'm weak and can't cope.
Having boundaries means I'm selfish and indulgent.
I may not want to do things, but I have to if I want
approval/safety/attention/love/validation.

We've encountered these very same limiting and self-defeating beliefs before! And we've also seen that they're just not accurate. If we want a happier, healthier life for ourselves, we need to seriously challenge these underlying assumptions, or nothing will change.

Here are five tips to help you make that mindset shift one day at a time:

Reframe What You Are Keeping OUT with Your Boundary

When you erect a boundary, *it's to keep away things you don't want in your life.*
You are not punishing anyone or pushing away something that is good for you.

If you're worried that having a boundary will offend or alienate people, consider this: anyone who doesn't respect a natural and reasonable boundary is not someone you want in your life in the first place! It is no prize to figure out how to manipulate yourself in order to keep such a person in your world.

If you have poor boundaries, you actually end up attracting precisely the kind of people who like pushing boundaries. If you forfeit your own needs, you will find plenty of people around you who are happy to follow your lead and do the same.

A boundary keeps out anyone or anything that will make never-ending demands on you. That's a good thing. The next time you're hesitant about saying no or drawing a limit because you worry that you're putting someone on the other side of the line, remind yourself that this is behavior you *want* to put on the other side of the line. Draw a line and put stress, obligation, guilt, and fear on the other side of it.

Mindset shift: "If I turn him down, **he'll** be offended," could be, "If I turn him down, **I'll** feel less pressured and won't have to deal with that feeling of guilt/obligation anymore, and I'll feel more confident in myself and what I really want." You're not keeping a good thing out (this man's approval) but keeping a good thing in (your own self-confidence) and a bad thing out (his potential offense).

Trust Your Feelings

People-pleasers love dismissing their intuition, downplaying their emotions, and assuming that their reactions are silly, inaccurate, or disproportionate. It's all just a way of saying, "My feelings don't matter." They do matter! Your feelings matter because they allow you to recognize your own wants, needs, and limitations. They alert you to the fact of a potential boundary violation and let you know when you are pushing yourself too far.

Your habit may be to quickly squash down any feelings of anger, fear, exhaustion, or disappointment. But instead, you could welcome these feelings and choose to listen to what they're telling you. No, this doesn't mean you lose control and let your feelings flood you; it just means you respect them. This teaches others to respect them, too.

Trusting and naming your feelings is work nobody else can do for you.

Mindset shift: After someone invades your privacy, for example, and you feel a pang of anger, instead of swallowing this anger and saying, "Oh, it's nothing, don't worry," you acknowledge your feelings and calmly say, "Actually, I'm not happy that you did that."

Your feeling of anger is the foundation on which you build your boundary. Without it, you are left floundering, trying to be "polite" and getting nowhere.

Respect Other People's Boundaries

It may not be nice to hear, but people-pleasers can often be the worst offenders when it comes to walking over the boundaries of others. If we routinely dismiss our own needs, it's actually easier to do the same to other peoples'. Our relationship with ourselves is always mirrored in the relationships we have with others.

Person A could fail to establish a clear and solid boundary by not properly communicating their limits—for example,

they fail to say, "I don't like you dumping your emotional baggage on me."
Person B then violates that boundary, i.e., dumps a whole lot of emotional baggage on Person A.
Person A is upset but, again, doesn't communicate this feeling. They lash out at Person B—and in doing so, they break Person B's boundary, in turn. Person A gets so frustrated that they share details of Person B's life with someone else, encouraging gossip and violating Person B's trust.

Having poor boundaries is not just a private matter. The way we conduct ourselves is reflected in our relationships with others, and our attitude ripples out to influence our broader workplace cultures, families, and communities. Work at respecting and being grateful for other people's clear and healthy boundaries. Practice what you preach.

Mindset shift: Instead of quietly thinking, "They always push me around, so they owe me, and that means I don't really have to respect *their* boundaries," think, "Respect is not a transaction or a bargaining chip. I accept other people's boundaries gladly because it's nothing less than I would expect for myself."

Give up Explaining

People-pleasers, at their core, secretly feel that they don't quite deserve to take up as much space as everyone else.

For this, they apologize, and their apologies take the form of "explaining" and justifying their feelings, their actions, their choices. To whom? To the people they believe do deserve it. In other words, people-pleasers may make the unconscious assumption that the *default* is for them to put others first, and any time they don't, they better explain themselves and have a good reason for doing so!

"I can't help out with the fundraiser, I'm so sorry. I've been having an awful time with my mental health lately, and really, it's because I've taken too much on. I ordinarily would have said yes, but I'm pretty exhausted, and I think it might have something to do with the cold I caught two weeks back..."

When you first start setting healthier boundaries, you may discover that there are lots of genuine *reasons* to have them. But then you may have another insight: you also deserve to have a boundary for no reason at all! And even if you do have a reason, you're not required to offer it to the other person. You can say no just because you want to say no, and you don't owe anyone a long justification. You especially don't want to get trapped into inappropriate oversharing.

Say no, then stop talking. Assert your boundary, and just hold that boundary. Justifications often sound like excuses to other people, anyway, because unconsciously they will hear the hidden apology.

Mindset shift: "I have to tell them all the reasons I'm *not* doing what they want me to do" becomes "Is there any reason *to* do it?"

Acquiescing endlessly to other people's demands is not your default setting.

Follow up with Action

It can be scary asserting a boundary.

Let's say you have a demanding friend who always invites you out but pushes you to come on inconvenient days to places you don't really like, and where half the time, you end up paying because they "forget" their wallet at home. This friend is constantly using you as free therapy, and you're frankly a little fed up with the endless "emotion dumps" (hello, it's Person B again). You decide to set some boundaries. For example:

"I have work in the morning so I can't do a late night, I'm afraid!"
"I've been overspending on nights out lately. Would you like to do something that doesn't cost anything, instead? Let's do that hike we keep talking about."
"I'm sorry, can we talk about something else?"

Most people mean well. If you set a reasonable and valid boundary with calm conviction, most people will respect it, even if it does take a few tries.

But that's *most* people—some people will see your boundary and walk right past it. What then?
Implicit in any boundary is a soft ultimatum. You are announcing your limits,

your desires, and the terms of engagement, i.e., the rules you have in place for how you interact with others. There is nothing wrong with this—we all have conditions on which we'll engage with others. If those conditions aren't met, we stop engaging, end of story.

It can be helpful to literally sit down and draw up a list of "dealbreakers" for engaging with you. For example:

I won't tolerate lying.
I won't spend too much time on people who have no genuine interest in me as a person.
I will never allow someone to belittle me or call me names.

You don't have to communicate these rules. You just have to know what they are, set your boundaries, and then, if those boundaries are violated, **act**. And yes, acting may mean reducing contact with that person. It may even mean permanently ending a relationship. For a people-pleaser, this can look like a scary outcome, but remind yourself that if someone repeatedly violates a clearly communicated boundary, then it is not you who is de-valuing your relationship, but them.

Mindset shift: You could say, "It will be a disaster if I have to put my foot down or end a relationship." Or you could say, "I don't have to continue engaging with people who don't respect me. The disaster would be to know I deserve respect . . . and continue to tolerate a situation where I know I won't get it."

Boundary-setting seems hard when you're not used to it, but it's actually really simple.

1. Identify your need or limit
2. Communicate it clearly in terms of that need (not in terms of the other's behavior, just in terms of your own need)
3. Behave accordingly (i.e., if the boundary is not respected, take action)

For example:

1. "I need to have enough rest and free time."
2. "I don't check my emails in the evenings or during weekends, as that's when I'm off work."
3. Set an automatic reply for your out-of-office hours, and commit to only

replying to emails or answering calls during work hours.

A boundary is easy to understand when you think of it as a rule you have for yourself and the "rules" on which your world runs. It's not a demand on others' behavior, a threat, a justification, a plea, or a punishment. It's an assertion about the standards you hold for yourself. Once you realize this, things become so much simpler.

Chapter 7: Being Assertive—or at Least How to Fake it till You Make It

Think of someone you consider assertive. How do you think they act?

We've spoken about how to verbally assert your boundaries and say no, but sometimes we need to simply **be** assertive. For example, the person pushing in front of us in the checkout line doesn't give us time to verbally respond—we need to be physically assertive enough to hold our ground. Even if we do say a few words like "excuse me," we need to make sure we're also sending the right nonverbal message loud and clear.

In 2019, Matthew Berry and Steven Brown did research on the vocal tones that actors employ when they want to play the role of someone who is assertive. Using "method" acting, these actors try to literally become the person they are portraying, changing their dress, posture, voice, and style of gesture accordingly. These outward mannerisms may seem superficial, but any good actor will tell you that they are powerful ways to control how others see you.

Imagine someone who says the lines, "No, I can't do that." Someone could utter these words with the cocky, self-assured demeanor of Indiana Jones staring down a baddie, or they could say them like Milhouse from *The Simpsons* who's just about to be punched by Nelson the bully. The words we say are often less important than the *way* those words are delivered.

Through their experiments (published in the *Journal of Experimental Psychology*), Berry and Brown discovered that there are nine character types that vary in their degree of both assertiveness and cooperativeness.

- Bully: High assertiveness, low cooperativeness

- King or Queen: High assertiveness, medium cooperativeness
- Hero or Heroine: High assertiveness, high cooperativeness
- Cynic: Medium assertiveness, low cooperativeness
- Self-portrayal (not acting): Medium assertiveness, medium cooperativeness
- Librarian: Medium assertiveness, high cooperativeness
- Recluse: Low assertiveness, low cooperativeness
- Loner: Low assertiveness, medium cooperativeness
- Lover: Low assertiveness, high cooperativeness

For our purposes, both the "lover" and the "loner" could also be considered pushovers or people-pleasers since they are minimally assertive and keen on cooperating no matter what.

Berry and Brown asked actors to give a performance based only on the above character descriptions, then analyzed audio and video of these actors, compared to the baseline where the actors essentially played themselves. The researchers discovered that the most important communicators of assertiveness were:

- Pitch, loudness, and timbre of voice (timbre here being wavering or stable)
- Speed of speech
- Continuity (i.e., how many pauses or breaks there were)

Based on their findings, **they settled on six acting techniques that strongly conveyed a sense of assertiveness.** Here's what they found:

Raise the pitch of your voice – Do so without going into unnatural falsetto.

Raise the volume of your voice – Don't yell, but speak up loud and clear.

Speak clearly and unwaveringly – In other words, keep a calm voice that doesn't wobble!

Increase the speed of your speech – This shows you know what you want.

Reduce the number of pauses – Especially drop "um" and "like."

Vary your pitch and volume – Instead of a monotone, allow your voice to go up and down, and to vary in loudness. This communicates that you are in control of your voice and therefore yourself.

If you doubt that these simple tricks could really make you appear more assertive than you actually feel, then you should try it out for yourself. Practice in front of a mirror and try to deliver a little monologue just as the actors in the experiment did, and include all six elements. Try again to say the same thing but do the opposite. Speak in a low, slow, wavering mumble that breaks often, and notice not only how it comes across but how *you* feel speaking that way.

It's not just your voice that matters, though. Your entire body is constantly communicating information to those around you, so it's worth making sure it's saying what you want it to! Jo Emerson is a confidence coach and explains that "acting 'as if' means you consider what qualities you would like to embody as a confident version of you—your best self—and then start acting in ways that echo this. For example, you might think your best self would smile at everyone you meet, in which case this is what you need to practice until it becomes second nature."

She, too, believes that people should "fake it till they make it"!

Doing this is easier than it looks, partly because it sets up a "virtuous cycle." The more assertive you appear, the more people will treat you as though you *are* assertive, and this positive feedback will give you more genuine confidence so that one day, you may find that you're not acting anymore!

Here are a few things you can try to fake it until you make it.

Watch Your Body Language

Comfortably take up the space you need. Take a deep breath and drop your shoulders, unclench the muscles of your jaw, and anchor your feet more firmly on the ground. Think about opening and expanding your body. When feeling confident, assertive, and even dominant, almost all animals hold themselves proudly and without hunching, cowering, or tightening any part of their bodies.

If you can manage this, you may find something interesting happens: when the muscles of your body relax, so, too, do your lungs, and your breathing rate slows. When you breathe deep and slow, your voice settles, and it's suddenly easier to speak in the way described above—with firm, steady conviction.

Stand up straight, lean forward, and keep your chin up. Slow down your movements and try to reduce fidgeting—especially in your hands. Keep them relaxed, loose, and open. If you shake hands with someone, do it firmly and paired with a smile-and-eye-contact combo. If you're ever unsure what to do with yourself, a good rule of thumb is to try to match and mirror the body language of those around you.

Maintain Comfortable Eye Contact

Your gaze is arguably the most fundamental and easily understood form of body language. Think of your gaze as a physiological manifestation of your will or intention. If you find yourself squirming to avoid eye contact or flittering your gaze all over the place, you may convey a sense of nervousness, indecision, or fear. People who can "look you in the eye" are also perceived as more trustworthy.

Instead, smile while you maintain eye contact and hold your gaze for around three counts. If you find eye contact makes you feel a bit awkward or is too intimate, it may help to switch your gaze from either eye and then down to the nose and mouth before switching back again.

Dress the Part

Karen Pine is a university professor and author of bestseller *Mind What You Wear*. She found that there is truth in the idea that you can "dress for success." But here, it's important to note that dressing well doesn't mean forcing yourself into a costume that doesn't have anything to do with who you are as a person. If you merely copy what you think is supposed to look good, you risk merely communicating how uncomfortable you are.

Dress as yourself but the best version, whatever that looks like for you. Make sure your clothes are always clean, in good repair, and ironed. Wear things that make you feel good. It's not about fashion but about presenting the visual version of yourself that you're most proud of.

You might need to spend a little time homing in on your personal style and considering your unique environment and context. It may at first seem superficial to try to be more assertive by simply changing what you wear, but when you get it right and you feel like a million bucks, it all makes sense!

Develop Your Personal Sense of Poise

Why do some people exude a sense of calm charisma? Why do some people seem so composed and in control? Such people dress, speak, and behave in entirely unique ways. This tells you that their aura of confidence is not about following a fixed set of arbitrary rules. Rather, it comes from within. **Poise and self-assuredness come from being aligned within yourself.** In other words, you are comfortable in your own skin, and people can tell. Following the tips and exercises in this book will hopefully help you cultivate this sense in yourself, but here are a few pointers in the meantime:

- Gracefully accept compliments. Say "thank you" and smile, and don't rush in to counter what's been said or think of something nice to say in return.
- Don't gossip about others or complain loudly about things that can't be changed. This communicates an attitude of insecurity and passiveness.
- Don't interrupt people. Relax into conversation, knowing you never need to perform, impress, or convince anyone. It will make you a better conversationalist, and you'll appear more confident in yourself.
- Try to avoid handing responsibility over to others, i.e., "Oh, I'm easy. I don't know, what do *you* want to do?" It's not very assertive . . . and it's annoying to boot!
- Breathe and pause. Slow down. You don't have to respond to everything immediately. Take your time and don't be rushed by anything. It conveys a wonderful sense of self-assuredness.

Chapter 8: Assertive Communication—Speak Loud, Speak Clear, and Speak from the Heart

Human beings are social animals. Plus, we all have needs. **Communication is our interaction with other human beings *in an attempt to have our needs met.*** However, the style of our communication reflects how well we understand, communicate, and meet those needs. Because communication and needs go hand in hand, having a problem with people-pleasing means it's likely you also have a problem with direct, healthy communication.

Aggressive communication means trying to get our needs met by yelling, forcing, coercing, intimidating, criticizing, or violating others' boundaries.

Passive (or passive-aggressive) communication means trying to get our needs met indirectly by manipulation, silent treatment, playing victim, avoiding conflict to win approval, or waiting around until others feel guilted into giving us what we need.

Both are attempts to meet needs... but they are seldom successful. The point of improving our communication skills, then, is to ensure that we are *meeting our needs in the best way possible.*

Somewhere in the middle of those two extremes is healthy **assertive communication. This is where we are able to calmly, directly, and respectfully communicate our needs without violating boundaries or infringing on the needs of others**. In the world of the people-pleaser, needs are a zero-sum game, i.e., either they win or you do. Either you are happy or they are happy. But healthy assertive communication recognizes a third possibility: that *everyone* can comfortably get their needs met without anyone having to give up their rights.

If you master healthy assertive communication, you will feel far more understood by others and will find you no longer stew over old resentments or disappointments. Your relationships will instantly become less stressful and more respectful. Plus, as a happy side effect, you're more likely to get the things you want and need!

How do we communicate more assertively? Here are a few main principles to keep in mind and how we can apply these principles to everyday life.

Feelings Are Never Right or Wrong

If you're a people-pleaser, you may shy away from expressing your "negative" emotions because you feel they're wrong, or worry that other people will judge you for them. But emotions are never right or wrong; they just are. We can judge our actions, and we can certainly say something about how we *respond* to our own feelings and emotions, but in themselves, these feelings and emotions are neutral . . . even the ones we call negative.

This insight allows you to clearly and confidently state how you feel. You can express yourself without it making the other person wrong and without judging yourself, i.e., by apologizing for how you feel or carrying it with guilt or shame. When we know that emotions are neutral, we don't treat them as something to fear or resist or avoid. This way, they actually have a chance to do what emotions should do—flow on.

Remember, **no emotion is right or wrong. But how you express that emotion matters!**

For example, you may be afraid to take a risk that everyone is encouraging you to take (for example, launching a risky new business), but believe that it's wrong for you to feel this way. You could try to conceal your fear. But in hiding your real feelings, you don't communicate what you'd really like to others, and never get the chance to learn what that fear could be teaching you. You prevent yourself from saying no. You end up taking the risk, but it doesn't feel right, and the business fails.

Your inauthenticity and acting against your principles are a direct result of you telling yourself your fear is invalid. The feeling of fear wasn't the problem; the way you communicated that fear (or didn't!) is the problem.

People Are Responsible for Their Own Feelings

By now you've probably heard of the technique to use "I" statements when communicating. There is nothing magical about the word "I," however. It's simply a way to rephrase sentences so that you focus only on what is legitimately in your realm of control and responsibility: yourself.

Let's say you do acknowledge your feeling of fear about launching a risky new business, and you accept that it's not right or wrong to feel this way. The next thing to understand is that this feeling is nobody else's but yours. It would be aggressive communication to say,

"All of you are pressuring me and forcing me to do this, and you're making me scared!"

It would also be a mistake to go the passive communication route and say, "What do you think I should do?" (i.e., "I'm confused, and that's *your* problem to solve").

We need to avoid blaming people for our emotions. Nobody can ever make us feel a certain way. If we are disappointed, for example, then that is our feeling. To say "You've disappointed me," is making another person responsible for your feelings—and it's probably the worst habit you can have when it comes to communication.

Reframing your language so that you and you alone are responsible for your emotions takes practice. Try to see it as a simple exercise in saying what is. Share your emotions with others without trying to find a cause or pin the responsibility on anyone (or anything, for that matter).

Not great: "You've upset me."

A little better: "When you don't reply, it upsets me."

Much better: "I feel upset. Could you reply to me more quickly?"

Understand What the Goal of Communication Is

What is the goal of communication? Have you ever even asked yourself that question?

For some people, a conversation is an opportunity for them to convince others to think as they do. For others, it's a chance to boast, perform, or capture an audience who will agree and validate them. For yet others, a conversation is a competition or even a war to see who's best or who's "right."

All of these mindsets will lead to poor communication. You will find, however, that all your relationships improve when you understand *that the ultimate goal of communication is to connect with others.*

That means that your aim is to work together and find a harmonious balance and mutually satisfactory outcome. You either have a good conversation **with** the person in front of you, or you don't have one at all, period. This means that the backbone of all communication is empathy, genuine listening, and enough willingness to put our own egos aside at least half of the time!

If you think that being a people-pleaser means you don't have much of an ego, think again. It is the ego that wants to be liked, to be seen and validated, and to control a situation. And it is also the ego that relinquishes responsibility and puts someone else in charge out of fear. When you understand the real goal of communication, then you understand that engaging with others is not about making them happy, making you look good, being a victim, or playing a game of control.

Applying Self-Knowledge and Asking for What You Want

It is your responsibility to know who you are and what you want. It's also your responsibility to clearly and respectfully communicate that want to others. Remember that communication is a way to get your needs met, but it has to be done while maintaining harmonious and cooperative connections with others.

We can know and accept how we feel.

We can take responsibility for this feeling.

Then, while we maintain cooperative connections with others, we can ask for what we want and need.

Does this mean we are magically granted everything we request? Nope. But if we approach communication this way, we have the greatest chance of having our needs met. With self-knowledge, responsibility, and clear requests, we maintain our relationships and connections *even if* we disagree with others or find that there is conflict. That is valuable.

For a people-pleaser who is used to denying their feelings and downplaying their needs, it can be difficult to clearly and confidently ask for anything. But requests are like boundaries—we are all entitled to them. We are all at liberty to express our needs. Sure, it doesn't mean the other person always can or will meet those needs. But even if they don't, we still retain our dignity and composure.

Here's how to speak your mind, communicate your feelings, and ask for what you want:

1. Thoroughly understand and own your own feelings without judging them or placing blame or shame. Frame this feeling using "I" statements.
2. Express a desire for a mutual solution, harmony, and cooperation.
3. Clearly state what you need to happen—not what *they* should do, but what you need.

For example: "I'm feeling totally confused and stressed out by this new system. I know how hard you've worked to implement it, so I'm keen to find a way to make it work. What I need is a clearer list of tasks in one place. Could I ask that you create such a list for me?"

Notice how different this is from: "This weird new system of yours is driving me crazy. Why do you insist on fixing things that aren't broken? I guess we're all stuck with it now, so I'll just give up my weekend again to try and decipher it..."

This is passive aggressive. There is no responsibility taken for feelings, and the other person is blamed as the source of these feelings. There is no clear and direct request; instead, this person is going to whine and complain until someone guesses what they want and gives it to them . . .

Now consider this: "Your awful new system isn't working. You need to do something about it!"

This is just plain aggressive. No acknowledgement of feelings, no expression of goodwill or interest in a mutually satisfying outcome, plus no request—only a demand.

The first statement, however, shows you it's more than possible to clearly and directly ask for what you need without aggression and manipulation, and without damaging the underlying relationship. People-pleasers are already half on their way to great communication because they already understand the value of cooperation, empathy, and kindness. They simply need to learn to pair this with clear requests and a healthy understanding of their own emotions.

Takeaways:

- One of the most useful tools in the people-pleaser's survival kit is the ability to say NO. There are at least six different kinds of no to learn and practice: the direct no, the reasoned no, the reflecting no, the rain check no, the enquiring no, and the broken record no. Each can be used in different circumstances, according to the boundary you need to set. Whichever form you use, you'll need to challenge your assumptions and beliefs about saying no and communicate clearly and confidently.
- Everyone has a right to have boundaries. Try to reframe how you think of boundaries—they are there to protect and prioritize what's important, and not shut someone out or offend them. Trust your own feelings and judgments instead of avoiding them.
- State your boundary and don't overexplain or ask permission. Then, if a

boundary is violated, follow up with appropriate action. A big part of healthy boundaries is respecting other people's boundaries, too.
- Assertiveness is something you can fake till you make! Be mindful of your body language (stand tall and take up space), maintain comfortable eye contact, fine-tune your personal sense of style (whatever that is), and practice the habits of a poised, composed person (such as gracefully accepting compliments).
- Assertive communication is not about force or coercion (aggressive) or pandering and submission (passive-aggressive) but about speaking confidently from the heart. To achieve mature, healthy communication, remember that feelings are never right or wrong, but it matters what we do with those feelings.
- Other people are responsible for their feelings, and ultimately, the goal of communication is not to control others but to connect with them and get our mutual needs met. Finally, an important

skill is to ask for what you need from a position of self-knowledge.

Part 3: Changing Your Mindset for Good

Chapter 10: Don't Take Your Inner Critic's Word for It

Here's a story you may be familiar with:

Person A is trying to think of the perfect gift for Person B. Person A goes to great lengths to find just the right present, wrap it perfectly, and then give it to Person B. Almost immediately, though, Person A starts to think, "Maybe I spent too much on that gift . . . maybe Person B secretly hates it and is just too polite to say. What an idiot I was to assume they would like such a stupid gift! You'll never live it down; everyone is going to wonder why on earth you bought such a strange gift . . ."

Meanwhile, almost completely unnoticed by Person A is Person B, thinking, "Oh, cool! What a nice gift."

People-pleasers are often their own worst enemies. **People-pleasing behavior can stem not from the outside world but from a harsh inner critic—whose words may seldom correspond with actual reality!**

Sometimes people-pleasing can be an attempt to address the ongoing negative self-talk that is constantly self-critical and judgmental. The inner critic is like a reverse cheerleader and is there on the sidelines, constantly reinforcing the negative core beliefs you have about yourself and a catastrophic narrative about the world.

An inner critic is sometimes understood to be the internalized voice of a real-life critic we had in our early childhood experiences. In other words, if you're a people-pleaser today, you may have been a parent-pleaser in the past!

Trauma, abuse, rejection, and self-esteem issues can put us on the path of people-pleasing, where we start to believe that our worth and validation come solely from satisfying others. Children unconsciously absorb certain messages about who they are, and take on these beliefs for themselves in the form of the inner critic.

As adults, we continue the same dynamic but within ourselves. In place of the parent is now our own inner critic. Unless we satisfy that voice completely, we are worthless. The trouble is—the inner critic is *never* satisfied. The inner critic is, to put it mildly, a bully who is devoted to sabotaging you. It says things like:

You're not good enough.

You're a loser/a bad person/an idiot/ugly/talentless.

Whatever you do, it's going to turn out terribly.

You're to blame because you're bad and you messed up.

Face it—nobody actually loves you. And why would they?

Life can't improve for you, ever. You're a failure.

Just give up.

Who do you think you are, putting up boundaries and asking for your needs to be met?

Seeing the inner critic's script laid bare can be startling, but how many of us are carrying around beliefs exactly like this, day after day? How many of us have held on to beliefs like this for so long that we don't even notice we have them anymore? The thoughts have crystallized and become our reality. Become who we are.

Luckily, it's never too late to become aware of the inner critic, challenge it, and replace it with something that's more on our side.

Here are a few powerful questions to ask yourself whenever you notice that you're stressing out about pleasing someone else at your own expense.

"Is the Choice I'm Making for Me or for Someone Else?"
The trick here is that the "someone else" could be other people, but it also could be your inner critic! Are you acting from your own freely chosen conscious values and principles? Are you acting because doing so is genuinely what you want for yourself?

Or are you acting to appease someone, to please them, to win favor . . . and simply to get that guilty and judgmental inner voice to shut up?

If you do discover that you are acting for someone else, then just be aware of that for a moment. Why are you acting for them and not yourself? What will happen if you do? Is it a healthy and wise choice for you?

Without judgment, dig a little deeper and see if you identify what's feeding that belief and where it really comes from. Wouldn't you like to choose something different?

"Is My Inner Critic Working for Me or Against Me?"

Most of us are so used to taking our self-talk as gospel that we don't stop and assess its truth or its usefulness. If we can become conscious long enough to notice the inner critic at work, then we can challenge it. We can ask, "Wait a second, is this actually helping me in any way?"

Let's say you're a vegetarian at a restaurant, and you've just been mistakenly served a giant steak. The inner critic immediately steps in and says, "Keep your mouth shut. If you complain to the waiter, you'll look fussy and ungrateful, and everyone will think you're being difficult. Plus, you'll embarrass the poor waiter. Just smile and eat the salad. With your waistline, it's probably wise, anyway..."

But you can pause and become curious about this voice. Could you imagine yourself using this voice on someone you loved? No. This is not the voice of someone who wants to help. It's working against you. Could you challenge it? What would that inner voice look like if it had your best interests at heart, instead? Turning it around, what would you say to a loved one in your predicament?

"Oh well, it was an honest mistake, but I have to have something to eat. I'll politely ask for what I originally ordered. I deserve to have a nice meal out just like everybody else here, and I'm not doing anything wrong by correcting the mistake."

Every time you speak to yourself internally, you have the option of being for yourself or against yourself. You may have an inner critic, but we also all have the opportunity to choose instead to listen to the wiser, more conscious part of us that wants the best for us. The choice is yours.

"What is My Inner Critic Trying to Achieve?"

The inner critic is a saboteur, yes, but where did it come from? Why is it there?

Though it's hard to believe at times, the inner critic is actually attempting to help, in its own misguided way. In your childhood, the inner critic stepped in to try to keep you safe and help you make sense of the world.

For example, a young child who has been rejected by their parents may rightly wonder, "Why me? Why would they abandon me?" The inner critic steps in to try to make sense of a senseless situation. "They rejected you because you're not good enough." Sounds cruel, but this core belief actually allows you to survive because it tells you that if you only work hard to be good enough and make others happy, then you'll earn back the love you need. So, you grow up to be a people-pleaser.

It's not great, but it works. The inner critic did its best to help in a difficult situation. But as an adult, you can become aware of the fact that what worked in the past may no longer work anymore. You can look at this inner critic for what it is: not the voice of reality, but as an outdated and self-sabotaging coping mechanism.

In IFS (internal family systems), we see the psyche as a mini family with its own sub-personalities. For example, one part of you could be a confused, innocent child who doesn't understand why they've been rejected. Another part is the inner critic who steps in to manage those difficult feelings, albeit with the lie, "If you do everything right and please other people, then you'll be loved."

To apply the theory of IFS, simply identify these various parts of yourself and see them as separate parts of you. Literally imagine sitting down at a family table with all these parts. Imagine talking to each part and asking it where it came from and what it wants.

The goal is to consciously let go of old habits and behaviors that no longer serve you. The next time you hear your inner critic speak, you can calmly say to it, "Thank you, inner critic. I can see you're trying to help. But right now, I'm choosing to let the wiser, more mature part of myself take over. And she says I'm worthy of love just as I am right now."

This leads us to a great technique to use, inspired by IFS: see if you can identify the Inner Champion inside yourself, as someone who argues against the inner critic and bravely works for your interests. Your Inner Champion doesn't let the lie of your inner critic go by unchallenged, and they're always there with a more rational, compassionate, and simple antidote to the shame and fear the inner critic usually brings.

"You will never really understand why your parents did what they did, but no child deserves to be rejected, including you. People-pleasing was a young child's attempt to win love, but luckily for you, there are healthier ways to do that now as an adult—without people-pleasing!"

There is a part of you that is strong, conscious, creative, playful, and intelligent. Even though the voice may be tiny and quiet, it *is* there, and it does work against the inner critic and reminds you of your innate worth.

This part wants only the best for you. Tune into that part and ask it for its advice. What does it say about your negative self-talk? Does it have an alternative view that you might consider?

Chapter 11: How to Drop the People-Pleaser's Worst Habit—Over-Apologizing

"Sorry!"

"You sure do say sorry a lot."

"I know ... I'm sorry!"

It's a silly joke, but probably hits a little close to home for chronic people-pleasers.

Over-apologizing (or having an "over-apologizing compulsion") can have a wide range of causes, but the most common is the need to please others. Here are a few examples:

- You raise your hand in class to ask the teacher a question, but preface it with, "Sorry, but can I just ask ... "

- You apologize to the receptionist for calling to book an appointment. "Sorry to bother you, I know you're busy, but..." (as if that's not precisely what the receptionist's job is!).
- The person in front of you in the checkout line is taking a long time. You smile at the people behind you in the queue. "Sorry this is taking so long!"

But why do people over-apologize?

Over-apologizing comes from a complicated mix of low self-esteem, the desire to please others, awkwardness and discomfort, conflict avoidance, anxiety, and sometimes a big helping of perfectionism thrown in, too.

Sometimes, over-apologizing is just a bad habit. You've probably noticed that it's a kind of learned social behavior. For women especially, apologizing becomes a socialized way to signal submissiveness, compliance, cooperation, and even gratitude. We may be so used to apologizing that we do it on behalf of others, for things that haven't actually happened, or for things that we're not even in control of. We may apologize for nothing at all—for example, "Sorry, what's your name?"

The core beliefs informing the need to over-apologize are all the same ones we've already encountered in one form or another:

I'm responsible for other people or other people's emotions.

It's my job to meet people's needs (hence I need to apologize if I don't do what I "should").

It's my job to smooth things over and manage social situations.

Conflict is not permitted (even awkwardness or uncertainty is sometimes too much!).

I'm a bad person, and I usually do things wrong—so I'd better apologize in advance for all the ways I'm about to disappoint everyone!

Apologizing makes people think you're polite, nice, and likeable.

Saying sorry when you've done something wrong is admirable. But when you over-apologize, you actually dilute this sentiment instead of amplify it. You may appear to others as timid, weak, passive, and groveling. The irony is that you may elicit from people the very behavior that you're most trying to avoid! Worse still, you're at a loss for when you genuinely are remorseful and want to make amends—you have no words left since "sorry" is completely overused.

Luckily, over-apologizing is a bad habit that is not too difficult to break—once you know you're doing it. Here are a few tips.

Tip 1: Just keep quiet

Really. You can't say sorry if you're not talking! Pause before you apologize and double check—have you really done something wrong that you need to apologize for? If an apology is in order, it won't matter if you wait a few moments to deliver it.

If you feel yourself wanting to mutter those two little words, just become aware, bite your tongue, and say nothing instead. Notice, then, that the world usually tends to carry on as it was without your automatic contrition!

Tip 2: Show your compassion and kindness . . . just in a different way

Maybe the knee-jerk reaction to apologize is really a compulsion to show someone that you care and are paying attention to their needs. Luckily, there are other, more effective ways of communicating this message.

Every time you feel the urge to say "I'm sorry," just pause instead and ask yourself what sentiment you're really trying to express. Is it perhaps, "I realize how you must feel about XYZ," or, "I'm here for you if you need me"? Sometimes, we show our concern for others most when we simply keep quiet and show our willingness to listen.

If someone tells you their dog has just died, for example, resist the impulse to blurt out "I'm sorry!" Instead, ask how they're handling it, check if they want to talk, or simply be quiet and let them express what they want to express. This will probably make them feel much better than a knee-jerk apology.

Tip 3: Train a different automatic response

Sometimes, saying "I'm sorry" is just a verbal tic or something you say without thinking. People may be in the habit of using it to announce opinions—even those they are one hundred percent not sorry for. For example, "I'm sorry, but that's just bad behavior." Here, the word *sorry* is merely used as a filler, albeit a pretty useless one.

Instead, try to practice other habitual turns of phrase to replace *sorry*.

"I'm sorry, what did you just say?" or even just, "Sorry?" could be, "Could you please repeat that?"

"I'm sorry, but I can't understand putting pineapple on pizza," becomes, "I think pineapple on pizza is weird!"

"Sorry!" (Said when people bump into one another or a minor accident happens) can be a simple "Oops!" or, "Excuse me," and a smile.

Tip 4: Change apology into gratitude

If a friend has come to visit and had to endure a traffic jam on the way over, instead of saying, "I'm so sorry that happened!" say, "Thank you so much for coming to visit. I'm sure that traffic jam wasn't great..."

Sometimes the instinct to blurt out an apology is really a misguided way to express our thankfulness for something someone has done for us. Make things simple by expressing that gratitude directly. Instead of saying on your next Zoom meeting, "Sorry my voice is all croaky; I've got a horrible cold," say, "Thank you so much for agreeing to a Zoom call instead of having me come in today. It really helps!" Put yourself in the other person's shoes and ask, what is more valuable, to have someone's contrition and apology or to have their sincerely expressed gratitude?

Tip 5: Speak plainly

"Softening" the way we speak or using "hedging" language is a way to present things in a gentler, less confronting way. This is a good skill to have when you're being kind and diplomatic, but an over-apologizer tends to over-use soft, subservient, or uncertain language. "Sorry" becomes a big part of diluting everything you say.

Are you the kind of person who prefaces any idea, suggestion, boundary, or claim with an apology? "I'm sorry, but can I just quickly say something? If it's all right, I'd like to suggest XYZ, maybe. I don't know. Do you think that could work? Sorry if that doesn't make sense!"

This kind of language is not unlike a timid dog rolling onto its back in a gesture of submissiveness! The irony is that this language can actually irritate people or invite them to dismiss or ignore what you say. It's far better to speak plainly, directly, and with confidence. "I think we could do XYZ."

Constantly apologizing every time you voice an opinion (or worse, every time you assert a perfectly reasonable boundary) communicates to others that you are meek, unsure, and generally undeserving of the thing you're asking for.

Tip 6: Reframe your idea of politeness

Let's be clear: people apologize for a reason. Saying "I'm sorry" at the right time promotes trust, shows others that you are interested in harmonious social engagement, and smooths over frictions and misunderstandings. Politeness does matter.

However, ask yourself honestly if your apology is about being polite, or if it's really about *managing your own anxiety and discomfort levels.* You'll know that it's more about your own anxiety if you insist on apologizing, even when it isn't your fault and even when the other person doesn't seem to need or want your apology.

Try to think of politeness, manners, and etiquette in a different way: it isn't something you do to put *yourself* at ease and lessen your own anxiety, but rather something you do to lessen the anxiety of *others*. To be perfectly honest—effusive, unnecessary, and over-the-top apologies are seldom for the benefit of people receiving them. If you want to be polite, learn to manage your own anxieties and take your cue from others. If you really do feel an apology is warranted, give one (just one!) sincere apology and then move on, even if you still feel guilty or awkward. Remember, your feelings are your own to manage—don't put people in the position of feeling that it's their job to forgive you.

Tip 7: Imperfect is not wrong

Try to become mindful of what exactly you're apologizing about. If you invite guests over for dinner, then feed them a bad meal that promptly causes everyone to get food poisoning, this requires an apology. But if you invite them and one of the nine courses you planned for the evening isn't quite up to Michelin star standard, then you probably shouldn't apologize!

Give yourself permission to be imperfect. We never have to apologize for learning or being beginners. We shouldn't have to apologize for being in process, or for not knowing something that was not humanly possible to know. Try to lower the standard. Ask yourself, is what I've done *wrong*? Or is it just imperfect because I'm a human being and not a flawless god? Don't apologize for imperfect. Don't apologize when you've genuinely done your best.

Tip 8: Discern what is in your zone of control

For some people-pleasers, over-apologizing can be a symptom of accepting responsibility for things that are genuinely not under their control—especially the behavior of others. Have you ever apologized on someone else's behalf? This may be a sign that you have codependent tendencies, which means that you tend to wrongly assume responsibility for another person's life and wellbeing.

It's a wonderful thing to be tuned into the needs and emotional realities of other people, but it can go too far if you have begun to feel that it's your job to apologize for the bad behavior of other people ... or simply for external events that are outside your control. If you apologize for a rude relative, for example, pause and really become curious about the core beliefs informing your need to do this. Why do you feel the need to accept culpability for their behavior as though it were your own?

As you can see, there are a lot of different reasons for "sorry syndrome" to develop, so it's worth understanding exactly why this behavior exists in your world. It may just be because you're genuinely kind and care about others and want to be agreeable, or it may be because you lack self-esteem and faith in your own judgment. At the extreme end, chronic over-apologizing can even signal a kind of "sorry for existing" mentality, which points to deeper and more damaging core beliefs.

If you dig deeply, you may find that this behavior has its roots in childhood, where an apology is a kind of coping mechanism designed to avoid conflict, win approval, or pre-empt judgment and absolve yourself of possible wrongdoing. Here, compulsive over-apologizing can stem from a deep sense of shame. If over-apologizing is a big challenge for you, ask yourself the following questions:

When did you first learn to feel guilty for having needs or making honest mistakes?

In the past, what kind of things might you have learned to apologize for?

What are you really trying to say when you say, "I'm sorry"?

How have you managed conflict in the past?

What would you do differently if you believed that you are a worthy person who is just as important as everyone else.

Chapter 12: Plugging into the Energy Source of Self-Validation

When we engage in people-pleasing, we are trying to extract validation, approval, and liking from other people. However, **self-validation is the ability to provide all these things for ourselves**.

Self-validation means we accept our own experiences, thoughts, and feelings, and acknowledge them as valid. When we do that, we no longer need people on the outside to affirm us, grant us permission, or tell us who we are. Without the anchor of self-validation, we are constantly and desperately looking to others, in effect asking them, "Who am I?" or "Do *you* think I'm worthy?"

Being the unique person you are entails experiencing a range of complex emotions and thoughts, all of which you are fully entitled to have. As the individual you are, you are no more or less eligible to take up space in the world or to live as you need to live than others are. Plus, you are the only real expert on what living this way ultimately means!

Taking onboard other people's wisdom and knowledge is a great idea. However, being a people-pleaser means we dismiss *all* our own unique individuality and assume that other people's opinions, values, thoughts, and ideas are *always* more valuable than our own. You'll know that you lack self-validation if you've ever felt like you don't quite know what your opinion is . . . until you ask everyone else their opinion first!

If you can learn to self-validate (i.e., to see that your experience is just as valid as anyone else's), then you will have much less need to get that validation from others. You will be unplugging from the shallow and inconsistent supply of external validation and instead hooking up to a deeper, more sustainable and genuine source of wellbeing that is inside you.

You'll be able to:

- See both your strengths and limitations and calmly claim them both without judgment or shame
- Understand your needs and prioritize them
- Live by your own values and standards rather than follow along with other peoples'
- Set healthy boundaries and limits
- Be able to resist peer pressure
- Be kind to yourself
- Be honest about how you feel and accept it
- Have a stronger and more stable sense of identity
- Have faith in your own judgment of things even if nobody else agrees with you

You will naturally develop your own ability to self-validate as you practice some of the exercises in this book. But here are a few more ways to develop self-belief that doesn't depend on the fleeting approval of other people.

Step 1: Be Aware of What You Feel

As a people-pleaser, you're so used to focusing on other people's emotions that you can be a bit disconnected from your own. A good first step, then, is to become mindful of what is going on with you right now in the present moment.

How do you feel? Can you give a label to this emotion?
What thoughts are you having?
Have any core beliefs been activated?

By asking these questions, you are giving yourself the chance to reflect on your real, current experience and acknowledging that without blame or shame. Sometimes, it makes a world of difference just to literally tell yourself, "**I'm allowed to feel what I feel.**"

Being aware of feelings can sometimes be difficult for people-pleasers because we may believe that some feelings are bad or make us bad people. For example, we may feel angry but deliberately stuff down this feeling because we have a core belief that strong emotions are unacceptable. We may assume that our anger, sadness, confusion, or disappointment are an affront or a burden to other people, and so we conceal them . . . and lose touch with our own emotional reality in the process.

But there is nothing inherently wrong with emotions. For some people-pleasers, accepting emotions is difficult because they wrongly assume that acknowledging how you feel is the same as agreeing with it. But as we've already seen, it's **our response to emotions that matters**. Feeling angry is perfectly acceptable even if yelling at others or being rude isn't. The entire range of human emotion is normal and natural, and we can acknowledge and validate that fact. That doesn't mean that we necessarily enjoy those emotions, that we approve of them, or that we want them to stick around. It doesn't mean we blindly allow our feelings to force us to act in ways we don't want to. And it doesn't mean that we make those feelings the basis of our personality.

This, then, is the challenge for people-pleasers: to find that healthy, stable spot right in the middle where we comfortably acknowledge how we feel while taking responsibility for how we act. From a graceful acceptance of how you actually feel, you can act in a way that reflects your values.

If you only fight against your emotions or judge them, you lose out on this chance to build self-knowledge as well as self-control. Plus, it's pretty stressful to always push back against your genuine experience!

- Be present no matter what the emotion is.
- Don't cling to an emotion or push it away.
- Don't try to look for a justification, ignore an emotion, or try to hurry it along.
- Just be there, with the emotion as it is. That's all. No Inner Critic, no interpretation, no judgment, no shame.

With practice, you may start to notice that your emotion is usually coming from a memory in the past, an old habit, or an ingrained assumption. You may notice that your tendency to apologize, invalidate, or second-guess is actually just a learned response and not a genuine and spontaneous reaction to the present.

If you can do this, you achieve half the work of self-validation, which is simply to give yourself space to be as you actually are!

Example: Ellie's boyfriend has announced that his ex is coming to town and he's going to have a drink with her after work. Ellie instantly feels crushed with doubt and jealousy, wondering what this all means.

After telling her boyfriend, "I'm fine with it, really!" a million times, she realizes she really *isn't* fine. She pauses and looks within, trying to name what she feels. There's a strange tight lump at the back of her throat, and she feels panicked and tearful. But she also notices that she wants to flee this feeling and to deny having it, especially to her boyfriend. She just notices and holds these feelings, however unpleasant they are.

Step 2: Normalize

Be aware of how you feel and then normalize that feeling.

It can seem difficult to do lofty things like accept, acknowledge, and embrace your emotional experience. But really, you don't need to do anything more complicated than understand that how you feel is normal and not a big deal. You don't have to beat yourself up, but you also don't have to suddenly declare that you love yourself unconditionally and are completely enlightened and stress-free (mostly, this would be a lie!). All you need to self-validate is the understanding that you're okay just as you are.

You're a human being with good and bad qualities. Everyone has emotions of all kinds, and everyone struggles from time to time. Nobody is so well-adjusted and content in themselves that they aren't hurt by a loss or intimidated by a challenge. That's simply part of life. Therefore, if you are feeling sad or confused or angry or hopeless or any emotion at all, chances are that other people have felt the same way, too.

No, you might not like experiencing these emotions. But to self-validate, you can "hold" them without needing to run away from how you feel or look to others to validate and approve of you.

Example: Ellie realizes that some old core beliefs from childhood have reared their head, i.e., "If you're too difficult or 'high maintenance,' then men will leave you." Ellie realizes she's judged her genuine feelings of fear and jealousy and instead chosen to people-please. But when she takes the time to normalize the emotion she notices in herself, she realizes that jealousy is not out of the ordinary in a situation like this, and that she is not being unusual, demanding, or fussy by feeling this way.

Step 3: Tell the Truth

One major way to break the spell of people-pleasing is to embrace radical genuineness. When you self-validate, **you trust yourself and your truth**. That means that you don't feel the need to lie even if it would be more convenient to do so.

"Lie" here doesn't just mean being deceitful, but also living inauthentically, hiding who you are, or agreeing to things that you don't really want to agree with. Simply, when you deny or reject certain parts of your genuine experience, then what you are doing is invalidating yourself. And when you do that, the door is wide open for others to invalidate you, too.

Instead, try to behave with a deep, real honesty and express yourself genuinely. People-pleasing is a quick fix to feel better, but we only feel truly good about ourselves when we are at peace with the truth of who we are. This all might sound quite intense, but it's at the heart of the mindset shift that helps you untangle from the needs and experiences of others and get more clearly in tune with your own.

Example: The next time Ellie's boyfriend asks her why she seems upset, she tells him honestly: she doesn't feel happy about him meeting his ex and is struggling with the idea. The two have an honest conversation, where Ellie doesn't apologize for how she feels, and neither does she rush in to try to people-please. From a place of self-validation, Ellie asks that her boyfriend cancels the meeting.

So what happens in Ellie's life once she identifies her emotions, normalizes them, and speaks that truth to those around her? Does she have a happily ever after? Well, maybe. But maybe not. Holding ourselves in high regard is no guarantee that others will. And gaining mastery and awareness over our experience doesn't necessarily mean that the experience magically goes away without any action on our part.

Whatever happens with Ellie, however, she has been true to herself. What her boyfriend chooses to do next is simply not up to her. It's up to him. But she has not violated her own boundaries or her values, she has not denied her genuine experience, and she has sincerely asked for a reasonable request. She also has not attempted to people-please, apologize, or resort to passive-aggressive manipulation ("I'm fine!" followed by weeks of obvious sulking).

Ellie can only do any of this because she is tapped into her own energy source of self-validation. She can say, "How I feel matters," and behave as though she really believes it. She doesn't need to worry herself about whether her boyfriend thinks her response is reasonable. She feels as she feels, and she trusts that.

Ellie may teach herself a valuable lesson: that **although making others feel good provides benefits, it is nothing compared to the sense of worth and dignity that comes from behaving with integrity.**

Takeaways:

- People-pleasing behavior can stem from a harsh inner critic, who is the one telling us that we are not worth anything unless we serve others, or that we do not deserve to have our needs met or boundaries respected.
- We can push against our inner critic by becoming aware of its voice and honestly answering some questions, such as: is the choice I'm making ultimately for me or for someone else? Is this voice in my head serving my interests or working against me? The inner critic, however, is there for a reason, and we can ask what that reason is. Seek to understand what that function is, then consciously choose to meet that need in a healthier way.
- People-pleasers often engage in self-sabotaging behavior: over-apologizing. This happens for many reasons, most commonly low self-esteem, the desire to please others, awkwardness and discomfort, conflict avoidance, anxiety, and perfectionism.
- To overcome over-apologizing, try to practice simply staying silent or expressing concern and compassion in different ways. You could also train out the "sorry habit" by expressing what you really mean to express—for example,

gratitude. Don't apologize for being imperfect, and reframe your idea of politeness so that it includes plain, honest, clear speech, which is always more truthful and assertive. Finally, don't apologize for things that are outside your control.
- When we engage in people-pleasing, we are trying to extract validation, approval, and liking from other people. However, self-validation is the ability to provide all these things for ourselves.
- We create self-validation when we acknowledge and accept how we feel without judgment, normalize that feeling, then speak the truth about it.

Part 4: Kind and Compassionate . . . But Not a Doormat!

Chapter 13: The Art of Compassion . . . REAL Compassion

As we move to the final part of this book, let's try to remember one thing: it's *wonderful* to be a "people-pleaser"—if by this we mean caring for others and being kind, considerate, compassionate, and helpful. We are, after all, human beings, and we are built to derive enormous satisfaction and meaning from connecting with others in this way.

But here is something that you might not have thought of before: **people-pleasers actually *lack* this capacity for true compassion and kindness.** That's because they are unable to cultivate compassion for themselves. It's because their attempts to care and contribute actually stem from a lack of love—for themselves.

Wanting to give, to take care of, and to cooperate with others is a noble thing . . . when it exists purely for its own sake. But for people-pleasers, this noble instinct has become all tangled up. Pleasing others becomes a transaction or a deal ("If I do what they want, they have to love me."), an obligation with fearful consequences, or an uncomfortable expression of low self-worth. It may even be an unconscious attempt to control others to manage anxiety. In other words, it's got nothing to do with love, kindness, or connection.

Many people might call you a big softie and urge you to toughen up and set boundaries, but perhaps your challenge is something else—i.e., to learn what *real* compassion looks like. In this chapter, we'll look at **mindfulness and loving-kindness practice as ways to help rescue our genuine compassion from our need to please.** These two forms of meditation are about expanding your perspective and opening yourself to a deeper and more authentic sense of worthiness, both in yourself and in others.

Mindfulness Meditation for People-Pleasers

You may already meditate for stress release or more conscious living, but **focusing on the present moment and nothing but the present moment** is also an excellent practice for a people-pleaser to develop. When you calmly embrace the moment without clinging or judgment, you:

- Become aware of your fleeting inner experiences and emotions instead of focusing on other peoples'. Most people-pleasers are great at avoiding or denying their emotions.
- Realize that life ticks along just fine without you needing to step in and take care of everyone's problems for them.
- Learn to **accept what is**. This means acknowledging and facing reality without the knee-jerk impulse to change it, save it, fix it, avoid it, judge it, hold on to it, etc.
- Develop better mind-body connection so that you genuinely feel your emotions rather than just talk about them abstractly.
- Gain space to let your genuine hopes and dreams emerge, and give yourself the opportunity to try on different perspectives without the pressure of adopting someone else's point of view.
- Finally, connect to something bigger than yourself—i.e., a spiritual dimension or God—that you can rest in. It's a feeling of knowing that not

everything is in your control and that you deserve love, too.

Mindfulness meditation is about one thing: presence. In this moment, as it is, right now.

When you immerse in it, you will notice that it is in fact a *loving* presence. There is a kind of calm, joyful acceptance of everything that emerges. It is filled with gratitude, curiosity, and creativity. That sense of being awake and aware to the glorious ever-unfolding moment is the soil in which real compassion grows. Once we can feel loving presence for the present moment, we can start directing it toward ourselves and others.

For the people-pleaser, love is something you earn. You have to DO something to get it, and the process is always a struggle or a compromise. But if love is something you win by your efforts, then that means that right now, you are not good enough just as you are for that love. This deep loathing will stay with you no matter how nice you are or how much you do. You trap yourself in a cycle that actually shuts you off from the very thing you want from others, not to mention from your own wisdom and self-love. This is a position of **fear**.

In mindfulness meditation, though, we are already worthy. There is no problem and nothing to do. We are whole and complete. There is nothing in the moment but open hearts and curious, non-judgmental attention. There is no need to negotiate and bargain with others for our self-worth because we are fully aware of the goodness in ourselves already. This is a position of **love and acceptance**.

Here's a simple exercise to try.

1. Sit somewhere comfortably, slow your breathing, and relax.
2. If worries, concerns, and anxious thoughts pop up, say hello to them but set them aside.
3. Focus calmly on your breathing, and immerse in all the many sensations it brings, without any labeling, judgment, or interpretation.
4. When distracting thoughts pop up again, set them aside again and come back to your breath.

And that's it. Now, something may happen where you hear yourself saying something like, "You're doing this wrong." Well, see this thought and accept it, too. Fine, do it wrong. So what? Come back to the breath. "This is boring." Okay. It's boring. Come back to the breath anyway.

Worrying about doing things perfectly is a form of people-pleasing, right? But when you notice yourself *trying to do something*, then you're not meditating anymore. So just stop. Don't try. There is nothing to achieve, anyway! Don't give in to the thought, but don't fight it, either. Just pull your attention away from it and focus again on the present and your breath in it. That's all. You don't have to figure out any big cosmic secret or claw your way to enlightenment or become good. Everything is already done; you just have to sit here and be.

Mindfulness meditation is not just something to do on a cushion for ten minutes a day, though. Done right, it should punctuate as much of your day as possible. Whenever you can, just pause what you're doing and become aware again. Sink into your senses, be still in yourself, and breathe. It is better to create a thousand tiny moments like this in a day than to achieve an hour-long meditation marathon.

Reconnect to the moment as you sip your coffee, or as you do a yoga stretch on your way out the door. Listen to the birds. Even if you have some negative and difficult emotions come up, see if you can adopt that calm, accepting attitude and look at these negative emotions so that you just see them as is without judgment.

Bringing moments of softness and calm into your everyday life will gradually teach you that you are enough, and there is enough. The moment around you is sufficient, and there is nothing you can or should do to earn your place in it.

Loving-Kindness Meditation for People-Pleasers

The awareness you develop is not cold and neutral—but warm, open-hearted, and accepting. With the following exercise, you practice opening up to receiving this compassion and also giving it to others with "no strings" and no conditions.

Before we jump in, a few caveats: when we have compassion for someone, it's not the same as agreeing with them or admiring them or thinking that they're better than us. We don't have to forgive them or understand them. We don't even have to like them. Compassion is simply the recognition that another human being has their own innate worth simply by virtue of them being alive and part of what is.

When we extend compassion to others, we don't pretend they have no faults or that we like their faults. We just accept them because that's what they are. We accept the moment as it is, and we accept the people we find in it. Think of compassion as total acceptance, but with a warm glow! We do not have compassion because people have earned it and deserve it, or because we want to play at being saints. We just see people for who they are and hold them in our kind awareness.

Step 1: First, relax and get ready for your meditation. You could try the above mindfulness meditation for a few moments, or do some yoga stretches.

Step 2: Use visualization to imagine what "compassion" looks like. Maybe a glowing pink orb emanating from your heart, or a kind little bird. Imagine yourself creating and holding on to this compassion.

Step 3: Now think of someone you love dearly. Imagine bathing them in this pink light, holding them in a compassionate embrace, or whatever other visual imagery you'd like to create. Extend this feeling to them. Or imagine the little bird dancing above their heads, singing a song. See them smiling and laughing, and feel your kindness toward them. This is not abstract—really *feel* that compassion for real. Say, "May you be happy and well."

Step 4: Next, think of another person you like and extend the same compassion to them, and the same words. "May you be happy and well." Conjure the same feelings of warmth and kindness.

Step 5: Next, imagine someone you're just neutral about, and do the same thing. This may be trickier, but imagine them as children, or try to picture that there is someone out there who loves them just as you love your nearest and dearest.

Step 6: Move to someone you dislike, and then finally to someone you may even hate or fear. This will be challenging, but try it, anyway. See that they, too, are worthy of compassion. Bathe them in the light of kindness and tell them, "May you be happy and well."

Step 7: You're not done yet. The final (and maybe hardest!) step is to turn inward and give yourself that loving and compassionate awareness. See yourself as someone who loves you would see you. Look at all of you—your good, your bad—and accept it all with easy warmth and joy. Aren't you a worthy being just as you are? "May I be happy and well." Try to really feel what that means.

Loving-kindness meditation is a little different from other forms because we are not just cultivating awareness, but *loving* awareness. If you're a recovering people-pleaser, be on the lookout for any time you want to put *conditions* on the loving acceptance you extend to yourself or others.

For example, if you notice that you're finding it hard to feel warm about someone who has treated you badly, and then you notice the thought, "You're bad for not being more compassionate toward them; you're not being compassionate enough," then stop and take a breath. Can you have compassion for yourself right now, and the fact that *just as you are, you are still worthy of compassion*? Can you accept that people aren't perfect, and neither are you, and it's all okay?

A little humor may help. You can probably think of someone you love, warts and all. You don't love them because they're perfect, right? Try to see yourself the same way: your flaws do not disqualify you from love and respect. You are still a valid, worthy human being. Another trick is to picture everyone you know as a child. We were all children once, and even if we're adults now, we all still need love and acceptance just as much as we needed it then.

Chapter 14: Breaking the Illusory Bonds of Codependency

Sometimes, people-pleasing is a symptom of a large cluster of behaviors called codependency.

The term was originally used in the 1950s by Alcoholics Anonymous to refer to the partners of people battling substance abuse—i.e., one person was dependent on the substance, and the other was co-dependent. Addiction therapists often noticed that non-addicted partners would often indirectly enable and support the addiction and the toxic patterns it created.

Today, the term applies to a broader range of behaviors **where a person is reliant on another, whether that's physically, emotionally, mentally, or even**

spiritually. It is a style of attachment and a pattern or dynamic that emerges between people and comes in many different forms in many different types of relationships. What they all have in common, though, is porous boundaries, a poor sense of self-identity, enmeshment, and a misplaced sense of responsibility.

In a codependent arrangement, there are two people:

- One is the giver, the other the taker.
- One chases and pursues, the other avoids and resists.
- One takes no responsibility for their actions, and the other agrees to take on that responsibility on their behalf.
- One person needs the other, and that person, in turn, needs to be needed.
- And frequently, one person plays the role of "problem," while the other person runs around in a panic, trying to solve that problem, make excuses, rescue them, or please them.

You'll know that codependency is part of your need to people-please if:

- You feel like you're always walking on eggshells.
- You're often checking in with the person or asking permission. You're always wondering what they'll think and what the consequence of certain actions will be for you.
- You're constantly apologizing to or for that person.
- You think of yourself as a savior, and love that person even though they hurt you.
- You'd do *anything* to avoid conflict or upset.
- Your people-pleasing or weak boundaries seem to be limited to this one person.
- Leaving this person doesn't feel like an option—because unconsciously you like that they need you.
- You're a shadow of your former self since you've known this person.
- You're constantly trying to figure out how to solve their problems for them.

Caring about other people is normal. But in codependent dynamics, there is an imbalance that is destructive or flat-out abusive. Consider an example.

Person A is battling late-stage cancer but is acting in a self-destructive way and neglecting to take care of themselves. Person B steps in and forms a romantic relationship with Person A, who promptly becomes abusive. Person A lashes out and treats Person B like less than garbage. Everyone looks on and wonders why on earth Person B doesn't leave. Person B says, "How could I? It's true love. Person A doesn't mean it. They're just sick and they're scared; it's not their fault."

What is really happening is that Person A's behavior is being supported and maintained by Person B's excuses and justifications. Because Person B actually enjoys being needed and playing the rescuer, there is no real reason to end the relationship. Person A escalates and tries to push Person B away with more and more extreme behavior, and Person B digs in their heels, even more convinced that they need to be the rescuer.

They are trapped in a loop, and one of the things keeping them in that loop is people-pleasing.

"If I tolerate endless bad behavior and do everything you say and never have a single need of my own, *then* will I deserve your love?"

Make Yourself Your New Rescue Project

Codependency (if you're in Person B's shoes, especially) can be tough to handle because it's difficult to be honest about your behavior and why it exists. You may say things like, "I'm just an extremely compassionate person," or, "If I don't help them, then who will?"

But become aware of when you're making excuses like this, and why. At the root of codependency is often the unacknowledged "need to be needed," or, to frame it a different way, "I only have value if I make someone else happy."

If you're one hundred percent honest with yourself, are there some people in your life who you have chosen to be giving and kind to in an unconscious bid to win their affection? Sometimes, we can gravitate toward people who we feel are struggling, precisely because we sense that they may need us more than others and therefore will be more indebted to us once we care for them.

These are difficult things to admit, especially because it weakens our idea of ourselves as a kind, even saintly person who is merely doing the right thing. However, at some point, if you've played martyr long enough, you may be forced to acknowledge that your care, generosity, and kindness are not good for the other person, and they are not good for you.

Then you can reorient your thinking: make *yourself* your priority and commit to taking full responsibility for yourself rather than for someone else. See your own self-esteem as the grandest project worth throwing yourself into. Save yourself! Here are a few baby steps to try to do just that:

Regularly do the "separation of tasks" exercise.

What is your responsibility, and what is theirs?

The classic co-dependent story is about a dutiful 50s husband who goes binge drinking and comes home in a destructive rage. His wife is terrified but quickly gets out of his way, knowing that to challenge him would result in an even bigger catastrophe. In the morning, the husband wakes up to find that everything he smashed has been quietly cleaned away, and breakfast is ready on the table, with his wife smiling sweetly at him.

As she watches him eat gratefully, she thinks, "What would he do without me? I'm probably the best wife in the world." For the husband, the problem of alcoholism is cleared away like the broken dishes, and he doesn't have to think about it. There are no consequences to drinking that his wife won't clean up.

The next day, she tells her friend about the incident. The friend says, "You have to leave him," but the wife has zero intention of doing that. She would prefer it if her friend had said, "Wow, he's lucky to have you!"

In a less 1950s example, if somebody has been bad at managing their own time, it doesn't automatically mean it's your responsibility to step in and fix things for them by rushing and doing the task for them. It's their responsibility. Likewise, if you say no to a request you can't fulfil, the other person's response is not your responsibility. Even if they yell, scream, cry, or threaten suicide—it's still not your job to agree to do something to make them feel better!

Gradually separate yourself.

Slowly ask what you'd like to do regardless of the other person's preferences or needs, then do it. Try to untangle your self-concept from their opinions, especially their opinions of you.

For example, if your partner can't come with you to dance class, that doesn't mean you never get to enjoy a dance class. Simply go alone or with someone else. It can take time to re-learn who you are and what you like outside of the other person, but you can figure it out one activity and choice at a time.

Become curious where your bad feelings come from.

The next time you feel rushed, anxious, or guilty, ask yourself, "Where does this feeling actually come from?" Sometimes, when our boundaries are weak, we end up taking on the emotional energy of other people and mistakenly thinking it's ours. We unconsciously take on the role of "emotion metabolizer" for other people. When you notice yourself feeling bad in any way, stop and become aware of when that feeling started, and why. Have you taken on an emotion that's not really yours to take on?

For example, your teenage child is going away on a school trip but has left packing to the last minute. You've nagged and nagged and tried to help, knowing that if things go wrong, they'll come running to you to fix it. You notice as the departure date gets closer that you are getting more and more anxious—the packing isn't done, and soon it will be too late.

But then you pause and realize that this is not your problem to solve. You see that your child is not anxious, yet you are! You can let it go, knowing that getting caught out with a badly packed bag is a lesson that they have to learn, and you can't learn it for them. You can choose to relax and let your child incur the consequences for their own behavior.

Stop making excuses.

People in codependent dynamics sometimes think of themselves as helpless victims. But they aren't! *A codependent dynamic only continues with the consent of both parties.* It can be challenging, but become conscious of when you're making excuses for the other person, or for the state of your toxic relationship. Notice all the things you say to yourself to explain away bad treatment, or why you cannot choose something better. Hidden in these excuses is your own consent.

For example, you might tell yourself and others that your terrible girlfriend is just free-spirited, and that she's really your soul mate and you've been sent to the earth specifically to teach her about the meaning of love (sounds corny, but how many people secretly think that their status as martyrs is somehow pre-ordained by the gods?). When she treats you badly, realize that you excusing her behavior is nothing more than you saying, "I'm okay with this. I consent to this."

If you can be honest, you will soon see that there is no reason at all to forego your boundaries, to put your needs a distant second, or to accept an unhealthy relationship. If you can see your justifications for what they are (your consent in disguise), then you understand that the only thing keeping you in a bad situation is . . . you.

Use a journal to discover the roots of your behavior.

Ask yourself the following questions, and be as honest as you can in your responses:

- *How healthy are your boundaries, and do you need to set better ones?*
- *Is there an area in your life where you give endlessly and yet never get anything in return?*
- *Are there any relationships in which you have taken on a martyr role?*
- *In what ways can you relinquish control right now and let other people make their own decisions?*
- *Can you identify some people who you are unconsciously trying to impress?*
- *Are there any unrealistic expectations driving your behavior? Are you being a perfectionist?*
- *Who can you ask for help and support?*

- *What does it feel like to trust your own thoughts and feelings right now? What are your own thoughts and feelings?*
- *Are you really helping the other person by taking responsibility for them? Or are you just enabling them?*

Working through your own thoughts in a journal will help dial down the intensity of other people's needs and reconnect you to your own. In fact, journaling for better self-knowledge is the theme of our next chapter.

Chapter 15: Charting Your Progress in Black and White

Writing down thoughts and feelings in a journal is an excellent way to get in touch with your experience, work through your options, and gain clarity—all in your own time and on your own terms.

Writing is perfect for people-pleasers because it slows everything down and lets you work through things outside of the heat of the moment. Some people read all the books and do all the exercises, but somehow in a real-life moment with another person, they instantly revert to old knee-jerk people-pleasing behaviors. Journaling is something that you can do privately, and the many tiny changes you instigate in yourself accumulate so that the next time you're facing a potentially difficult situation, you are better equipped to manage it differently.

The exercises, techniques, and mindset shifts outlined in this book are not designed to work magically overnight. While some of your progress will be swift and dramatic, other aspects of your tendency to people-please may be more stubborn and slow to change. For some, cultivating a rock-solid sense of self, good boundaries, and crystal-clear communication is a life's work and a challenge that is never really complete. Whatever the case, your journal can be a secret weapon. A journal is:

- A way to slow down and get a grip on what you're thinking and feeling
- A way to track and monitor your progress—if you set goals and recognize milestones, you can see how far you've come
- A place to explore childhood patterns, unpack core beliefs, and experiment with alternatives
- A record to remind you of all the things you value, as well as

> affirmations, goals, dreams, and guiding values and principles

What you put in your journal is entirely up to you. Almost all of the exercises discussed so far can be engaged with in written form. Get creative! You could write down an imagined dialogue between you and your inner child, or write at the top of each page an affirmation or mantra that really speaks to you.

Use your journal to add structure to your meditation practice; you could start and end each session with a journal entry noting any patterns. Finally, the "separation of tasks" exercise is definitely something that benefits from pen and paper.

Use a Journal and Be Your Own Therapist

Whatever you use your journal for, remember that it's there for you and your use only. Don't share what you write with others, and remind yourself that you're not trying to create something likeable or perfect or rational.

A journal is a tool, like an external secondary brain that helps support your personal development. If you're not finding it easy to get started with journaling, here are a few open-ended prompts to get the juices flowing. Begin with a sentence fragment and just allow yourself to write down whatever emerges, without judging or self-censoring:

I'm afraid of _____.

Taking care of people makes me feel _____.

People love me because _____.

I wish I could admit that _____.

If I'm not in control, then that means _____.

I secretly wish that _____.

The golden rule for my life is _____.

Other people should _____.

What I most love about myself is _____.

If I say no, then other people will _____.

My job in life is to _____.

Everyone thinks I'm _____.

Right now, in this moment, I am experiencing _____. I first felt this way _____.

My inner child is saying _____.

I want to say no to _____.

As you write to some of these prompts, remember that the goal is not to find the correct answer—there isn't one. The idea is also not to answer quickly and move on, either. These prompts are just the beginning. As you answer, notice what comes up for you. Notice which ones are easy to answer, which ones annoy you, and which you can't seem to answer at all. Notice if you're resisting or avoiding a particular question. Become curious what this means.

Write to the prompt, but then keep writing. Meditate on your answer and then write some more. This is because for people-pleasers, there may be quite a few layers of automatic answers that you think you "should" write down, but when you keep going, you discover what you genuinely think—and it may be a surprise! With accepting and non-judgmental awareness, keep looking deeper.

How to Use Affirmations

Some people hate the idea of affirmations because they remind them of the cheesy 80s self-help that first popularized the practice. To be frank, standing in front of a mirror and saying, "Every day and in every way, I'm getting better and better," just doesn't feel . . . true.

However, affirmations really can be a powerful tool for boosting self-esteem, cultivating self-love, and reducing the need to people-please. That is, if they're done correctly.

A people-pleaser may try to please even when there isn't anyone around to please! Their compliance, willingness to do the right thing, and desperate need for perfection and validation can actually make them self-help junkies. Such a person may not be attempting to please or appeal to any particular person, but may have a vague and constant sense of what they "should" be doing. And if they discover that they have low self-esteem, this becomes yet another stick with which to beat themselves up with, and they dutifully schedule in self-care practice and force themselves to say affirmations.

And then it doesn't work. Why? Because, again, it is self-care that comes from a place of self-hate. Just like compassion that comes from a place of anxiety and fear, it is a contradiction in terms. So, even if you say, "I am worthy of love. I'm a good person," it might mean nothing if unconsciously you are thinking, "If I can master this self-love thing, then I will finally deserve acceptance. If I can just stop being such a lame people-pleaser, then people will finally like me. I'm going to work really, really hard at my confidence and stop being so messed up, and then everything will be okay..."

It's just more of the same, right?

The best way to use affirmations is to make your own. If you cut and paste other people's words, you may just be substituting their perspective and intention for your own. So, how can you create your own affirmations? Well, your journal can help you.

Step 1: Look for themes

As you write in your journal, you'll eventually notice certain patterns and themes emerging. Pay attention to these. For example, working through the exercises above and noting down your responses, you start to see that there is a pattern of you never asking for help.

You explore this and discover that in childhood, your parents were so engrossed in their own problems that they always treated your needs as an annoying inconvenience. You always felt like your problems were minuscule compared to the struggles your parents had to contend with, and so you formed the belief that, "I don't matter and my problems don't matter. My concerns are silly and irrelevant."

You then notice that this belief shows up everywhere in adult life. In order to please others and get them to like you, you pretend to be happier than you are and fake coping. You never reveal the truth or show vulnerability. Consequently, you suffer alone, thinking that your problems are not worth anyone's time or attention.

Step 2: Condense these themes

Try to capture certain ideas, thoughts, feelings, assumptions, and beliefs and represent them simply. You could write a sentence or even flesh out an image or symbol in your mind's eye. In our example, maybe you settle on the image of a giant restaurant called Life, where everyone is seated and enjoying their meal, but you are the eternal waitress, serving meals while you go hungry. Or you may outline this feeling in a single core belief or "life rule"—"My needs are not important, and to have them is an unfair burden on other people, who might abandon me as a result."

Step 3: Invert

Everyone is unique in how they experience low self-esteem, anxiety, or the need to people-please. Everyone has had different childhood experiences and different assumptions, expectations, and beliefs about themselves and the world. This is one of the reasons other people's affirmations don't always work—they don't always speak to *your* unique condition.

Once you've identified your own unique and recurring people-pleasing patterns, however, you can consciously invert them. For example, we could invert the following:

"My needs are not important, and to have them is an unfair burden on other people, who might abandon me as a result."

One possible inversion is to say:

"My needs are as important as everyone else's. Truthfully expressing my needs will not harm anyone. The people who love me will want to help if they know I need it."

Or you could imagine that instead of Life being a demanding and busy restaurant, it's a warm home where a loving family is sitting down to a shared meal. Everyone helps cook, and everyone eats together. Everyone is entitled to eat what they need and enjoy it, knowing that them doing so doesn't cost anyone else a thing. Asking for your needs to be met is as simple as saying, "Pass the salt, please."

Going through these three steps needn't take very long. You'll arrive at tailor-made affirmations and counter-beliefs that most directly challenge your old patterns of thinking and feeling. These are the kind of affirmations that will never feel cheesy or forced.

That said, here are a few ideas that do tend to speak to those wrestling with the people-pleasing habit. Try to take the following and adjust or adapt them to make them your own:

- I am enough. What I do is good enough.

- Giving is good. Receiving is also good.
- My feelings are valid.
- I don't owe other people a solution to their problems.
- People-pleasing is just something I do; it is not who I am or always will be.
- I don't need to be perfect or have all the answers.
- I am not in charge of other people, and they are not in charge of me.
- It's okay not to focus on other people one hundred percent of the time.
- I can choose.
- I am resilient. Other people's rejection, judgment, or expectation doesn't define me.
- It is not possible to completely avoid all conflict.
- I don't have to do things for people to win their love.
- Mature adults love one another because they want to. Relationships are not transactions.
- It's normal to ask for help, and people around me enjoy making me happy.
- People have the right to ask; I have the right to refuse.
- I choose to relax.

- I am a worthy human being even if I'm not always "nice."
- I am sufficient just as I am.
- Other people's feelings are other people's feelings. Managing them is not my job.

There has been quite a lot of material covered in this book. Some of it will have applied to you, and some of it not. But if you can do the legwork and arrive at your own personal, condensed lessons (i.e., affirmations), you give yourself a special shortcut to hold on to once you're finished reading. Every time you open your journal and quickly read your affirmation or remind yourself of a particular symbol or image, you are strengthening new thought patterns.

Eventually, you may find that these ideas start to sink in, and you begin to believe them. You may look back on the early pages of your journal and compare them to the current ones, seeing how bit by bit, you have transformed your perspective.

In daily conversations or situations, you may find you no longer need to consciously remind yourself of the affirmation; instead, you catch yourself behaving as though it's already true. Perhaps you automatically say no to an unreasonable request, not because you know that you "should," but because it feels like the most natural thing in the world to do . . . for a person who loves themselves.

Good luck on your journey, wherever you are, and trust that reaching this point of calm, confident integrity is closer than you think.

Takeaways:

- Kindness and compassion are wonderful if they are genuine. People-pleasers need to learn to develop the skill of genuine kindness rather than acting out of fear, obligation, or a sense of transaction. Mindfulness and loving-kindness practice are two ways to help rescue genuine compassion from the need to please.
- Mindfulness meditation is about presence and being aware of the present moment without judgment or grasping. Go calm and quiet within, setting aside thoughts as they arrive and accepting what is without trying too hard to achieve any particular end.
- Loving-kindness meditation practices generating warm, accepting, and loving attention and extending it to others as

well as to yourself. Visualize kindness flowing to the people you love, then progressively to others, and finally to yourself. Compassion does not mean agreement or forgiveness, only that we can acknowledge that as human beings, we all have worth since we are part of *what is*.

- People-pleasers can sometimes fall into codependent relationships, where one person is reliant on another, whether that's physically, emotionally, mentally, or even spiritually. These toxic dynamics can only be broken when the person is able to re-prioritize themselves as their own "rescue project" and rewrite the core belief that they are only good people if they are needed. This requires understanding the roots of behavior and refusing to make excuses anymore.
- A journal can be a recovering people-pleaser's most powerful self-help tool. It slows your thoughts, keeps track of your progress, and helps you uncover patterns as well as develop your values and goals. Use writing prompts to guide self-exploration without judgment.
- Recurrent themes will emerge over time, and these can be inverted to create your own affirmations. These become like

useful shortcuts to guide and shape your journey to healthier boundaries, better communication, and stronger self-identity.

Summary Guide

PART 1: WHY ARE SOME PEOPLE PEOPLE-PLEASERS?

- People-pleasing is a complex learned behavior, but it can be understood and changed. One of the most common underlying causes is the need to be liked.
- We can counter this mindset by remembering we are like inkblots (i.e., what people see is about them, not about you) and understanding that your worth does not come from other people's approval.
- When you untangle yourself from other people's opinions and judgments, you free yourself to ask what YOU want, what you care about, and what you value. The "separation of tasks" exercise helps you to tease apart your responsibilities from other peoples'—their feelings are not your business.
- Over-giving stemming from fear of rejection is not genuine generosity. Break the cycle by changing the core belief: "I cannot survive rejection." Instead, court

rejection deliberately and teach yourself that it doesn't define you. Challenge your narratives with self-compassion, and focus on process, not outcome.
- People-pleasing is sometimes part of a bigger behavioral response to childhood trauma called "fawning," i.e., a flood of appeasing, soothing, and conciliatory behavior.
- You may need professional help to address a fawning habit, but you can also make strides by re-parenting yourself. This entails choosing to give to yourself now what you weren't given as a child. Reparenting also entails connecting with your values and principles, getting in tune with your own emotions, and learning to have fun!
- People-pleasers can be conflict avoidant, but this is actually a high-risk strategy, and you may gather resentments only to explode later ("gunnysacking"). Instead, use "and" instead of "but" in conversations, or try the "Five Whys" technique to get to the heart of what you're really avoiding.

PART 2: THE PEOPLE-PLEASER'S SURVIVAL KIT

- One of the most useful tools in the people-pleaser's survival kit is the ability to say NO. There are at least six different kinds of no to learn and practice: the direct no, the reasoned no, the reflecting no, the rain check no, the enquiring no, and the broken record no. Each can be used in different circumstances, according to the boundary you need to set. Whichever form you use, you'll need to challenge your assumptions and beliefs about saying no and communicate clearly and confidently.
- Everyone has a right to have boundaries. Try to reframe how you think of boundaries—they are there to protect and prioritize what's important, and not shut someone out or offend them. Trust your own feelings and judgments instead of avoiding them.
- State your boundary and don't overexplain or ask permission. Then, if a boundary is violated, follow up with

appropriate action. A big part of healthy boundaries is respecting other people's boundaries, too.

- Assertiveness is something you can fake till you make! Be mindful of your body language (stand tall and take up space), maintain comfortable eye contact, fine-tune your personal sense of style (whatever that is), and practice the habits of a poised, composed person (such as gracefully accepting compliments).
- Assertive communication is not about force or coercion (aggressive) or pandering and submission (passive-aggressive) but about speaking confidently from the heart. To achieve mature, healthy communication, remember that feelings are never right or wrong, but it matters what we do with those feelings.
- Other people are responsible for their feelings, and ultimately, the goal of communication is not to control others but to connect with them and get our mutual needs met. Finally, an important

skill is to ask for what you need from a position of self-knowledge.

PART 3: CHANGING YOUR MINDSET FOR GOOD

- People-pleasing behavior can stem from a harsh inner critic, who is the one telling us that we are not worth anything unless we serve others, or that we do not deserve to have our needs met or boundaries respected.
- We can push against our inner critic by becoming aware of its voice and honestly answering some questions, such as: is the choice I'm making ultimately for me or for someone else? Is this voice in my head serving my interests or working against me? The inner critic, however, is there for a reason, and we can ask what that reason is. Seek to understand what that function is, then consciously choose to meet that need in a healthier way.
- People-pleasers often engage in self-sabotaging behavior: over-apologizing. This happens for many reasons, most

commonly low self-esteem, the desire to please others, awkwardness and discomfort, conflict avoidance, anxiety, and perfectionism.
- To overcome over-apologizing, try to practice simply staying silent or expressing concern and compassion in different ways. You could also train out the "sorry habit" by expressing what you really mean to express—for example, gratitude. Don't apologize for being imperfect, and reframe your idea of politeness so that it includes plain, honest, clear speech, which is always more truthful and assertive. Finally, don't apologize for things that are outside your control.
- When we engage in people-pleasing, we are trying to extract validation, approval, and liking from other people. However, self-validation is the ability to provide all these things for ourselves.
- We create self-validation when we acknowledge and accept how we feel without judgment, normalize that feeling, then speak the truth about it.

PART 4: KIND AND COMPASSIONATE . . . BUT NOT A DOORMAT!

- Kindness and compassion are wonderful if they are genuine. People-pleasers need to learn to develop the skill of genuine kindness rather than acting out of fear, obligation, or a sense of transaction. Mindfulness and loving-kindness practice are two ways to help rescue genuine compassion from the need to please.
- Mindfulness meditation is about presence and being aware of the present moment without judgment or grasping. Go calm and quiet within, setting aside thoughts as they arrive and accepting what is without trying too hard to achieve any particular end.
- Loving-kindness meditation practices generating warm, accepting, and loving attention and extending it to others as well as to yourself. Visualize kindness flowing to the people you love, then progressively to others, and finally to yourself. Compassion does not mean agreement or forgiveness, only that we can acknowledge that as human beings,

we all have worth since we are part of *what is*.
- People-pleasers can sometimes fall into codependent relationships, where one person is reliant on another, whether that's physically, emotionally, mentally, or even spiritually. These toxic dynamics can only be broken when the person is able to re-prioritize themselves as their own "rescue project" and rewrite the core belief that they are only good people if they are needed. This requires understanding the roots of behavior and refusing to make excuses anymore.
- A journal can be a recovering people-pleaser's most powerful self-help tool. It slows your thoughts, keeps track of your progress, and helps you uncover patterns as well as develop your values and goals. Use writing prompts to guide self-exploration without judgment.
- Recurrent themes will emerge over time, and these can be inverted to create your own affirmations. These become like useful shortcuts to guide and shape your journey to healthier boundaries, better communication, and stronger self-identity.

www.ingramcontent.com/pod-product-compliance
Lightning Source LLC
Chambersburg PA
CBHW030231100526
44583CB00013BA/787